HOW TO NEGOTIATE EFFECTIVELY?

Published by:
Lotus Press Publishers & Distributors

HOW TO NEGOTIAT EFFECTIVELY ?

Sandeep Anand

Lotus PRESS

4735/22, Prakash Deep Building,
Ansari Road, Daryaganj,
New Delhi - 110002.

Lotus Press Publishers & Distributors
Unit No. 220, Second Floor, 4735/22, Prakash Deep Building,
Ansari Road, Darya Ganj, New Delhi-110002
Ph.: 011-23280047, 32903912, 09811838000
• E-mail: lotus_press@sify.com, www.lotuspress.co.in

How to Negotiate Effectively ?

ISBN: 978-81-8382-214-5

Published by: **Lotus Press** Publishers & Distributors New Delhi-110002
Printed at: Concept Imprint, Delhi

Preface

The word "negotiation" is derived from the Latin word "*negotium*". When one goes into a negotiation, he or she should take a personal inventory. How one feels about negotiation? Does one want to get it over fast? If so, one may give in too quickly, or give away too much. Or, does one want to win, no matter what the cost? If so, one may become adversarial and damage the relationship. At first, one is to know whom one is negotiating with before one begins. What's his or her negotiator's reputation as a conversationalist? It's not enough to know what one wants out of negotiation. One also needs to anticipate what the other party wants (double think). The smart negotiator always tries to anticipate, what the other party thinks one wants (triple think).

Negotiation is a dialogue, intended to resolve disputes to produce an agreement upon courses of action, to bargain for individual or collective advantages, or to craft outcomes to satisfy various interests. It is the primary method of alternative dispute resolution.

— ***Editor***

Preface

Contents

1

Art of Negotiation

Know Thyself

When you go into a negotiation, take a personal inventory. How do you feel about negotiation? Do you want to get it over fast? If so, you may give in too quickly, or give away too much. Or, do you want to win, no matter what the cost? If so, you may become adversarial and damage the relationship.

Do Your Homework

Know who you're negotiating with before you begin. What's his or her reputation as a negotiator? Win/Win model or Win/Lose model? Does the person want to negotiate with you, dread the negotiation or is this a neutral situation.

Practice Double and Think Triple

It's not enough to know what you want out of negotiation. You also need to anticipate what the other party wants (double think). The smart negotiator also tries to anticipate what the other party thinks you want (triple think).

Build Trust

Negotiation is a highly sophisticated form of communication. Without trust, there won't be communication. Instead you'll have manipulation and suspicion masquerading as communication. Be trustworthy. Honour your commitments. Tell the truth. Respect confidences.

Develop External Listening

Most people carry on an inner dialogue with themselves. When you're trying to communicate with someone else, this inner dialogue becomes a problem because you can't listen internally and externally at the same time. When you negotiate, turn off your inner voice and only listen externally. You won't miss important non-verbal messages, facial expressions of voice inflections, when you listen externally.

Move Beyond Positions

It's risky to make yourself vulnerable to someone. That's why in a negotiation you begin by stating your position. Later, when the trust has deepened, you and the other party can risk more honesty and identify your true interests. As a negotiator, it is your responsibility to ask questions that will uncover the needs or interests of the other party. If you've also done your job of creating a supportive climate, you're more likely to get honest answers.

Own Your Power

Don't assume that because the other party has one type of power, e.g. position power, that he or she is all powerful. That's giving away your power! Balance power by assessing the other parties source(s) of power, and then your own. While there are many sources of power, they all break down into two categories; internal power and external power. The former no one can take away from you and includes your personal power, level of self-esteem, and self-confidence. External power fluctuates with your situation. If you're laid off or demoted you can lose position power, for example. If new technology is introduced, you can lose your expertise power. Because the dynamics of power are so changeable, a negotiation is never dead. Be patient; the power dynamics may shift.

Know Your BATNA

BATNA stands for Best Alternative To a Negotiated Agreement. The acronym comes out of the research on negotiation conducted by the Harvard Negotiation Project. Before you begin a negotiation, know what your options are. Can you walk away from the deal? What other choices do you have? What are the pros and cons of each choice? Don't stop here. Also consider the BATNA of the other party.

Know What a Win Is?

What is your best case scenario? What is your worst case scenario? The area in between is called your settlement range. If you can reach an agreement within your settlement range, that's a Win! Don't drop below your bottom line; you'll feel bad about yourself and the deal afterwards, and you may not follow-through on your commitments.

Enjoy the Process

Negotiation is a process, not an event. There are predictable steps preparation, creating the climate, identifying interests, and selecting outcomes that you will go through in any negotiation. With practice, you will gain skill at facilitating each step of the process. As your skill increases, you'll discover that negotiating can be fun.

2

Concept and Perception of Negotiation

Negotiation is a dialogue intended to resolve disputes, to produce an agreement upon courses of action, to bargain for individual or collective advantage, or to craft outcomes to satisfy various interests. It is the primary method of alternative dispute resolution.

Negotiation occurs in business, non-profit organisations, government branches, legal proceedings, among nations and in personal situations such as marriage, divorce, parenting, and everyday life. The study of the subject is called *negotiation theory*. Those who work in negotiation professionally are called *negotiators*. Professional negotiators are often specialised, such as *union negotiators, leverage buy out negotiators, peace negotiators, hostage negotiators*, or may work under other titles, such as diplomats, legislators or brokers.

The Etymology

The word "negotiation" is from the Latin, *"negotium"*.

Approaches to Negotiation

Negotiation typically manifests itself with a trained negotiator acting on behalf of a particular organisation or position. It can be compared to mediation where a disinterested third party listens to each sides' arguments and attempts to help craft an agreement between the parties. It is also related to arbitration which, as with a legal proceeding, both sides make an argument as to the merits of their "case" and then the arbitrator decides the outcome for both parties.

Negotiation involves three basic elements: *process, behaviour* and *substance*. The process refers to how the parties negotiate: the context of the negotiations, the parties to the negotiations, the tactics used by the parties, and the sequence and stages in which all of these play out. Behaviour refers to the relationships among these parties, the communication between them and the styles they adopt. The substance refers to what the parties negotiate over: the agenda, the issues (positions and — more helpfully — interests), the options, and the agreement(s) reached at the end.

Skilled negotiators may use a variety of tactics ranging from negotiation hypnosis, to a straight forward presentation of demands or setting of preconditions to more deceptive approaches such as cherry picking. Intimidation and salami tactics may also play a part in swaying the outcome of negotiations.

Advocate's Approach

In the advocacy approach, a skilled negotiator usually serves as advocate for one party to the negotiation and attempts to obtain the most favourable outcomes possible for that party. In this process the negotiator attempts to determine the minimum outcome(s) the other party is (or parties are) willing to accept, then adjusts their demands accordingly. A "successful" negotiation in the advocacy approach is when the negotiator is able to obtain all or most of the outcomes their party desires, but without driving the other party to permanently break off negotiations, unless the best alternative to a negotiated agreement (BATNA) is acceptable.

Traditional negotiating is sometimes called *win-lose* because of the assumption of a fixed "pie", that one person's gain results in another person's loss. This is only true, however, if only a single issue needs to be resolved, such as a price in a simple sales negotiation.

The "Win/Win" Negotiator's Approach

During the early part of the 20th century, academics such as Mary Parker Follett developed ideas suggesting that agreement often can be reached if parties look not at their stated positions but rather at their underlying interests and requirements to reach a decision that benefits both parties.

During the 1960s, Gerard I. Nierenberg recognised the role of negotiation in resolving disputes in personal, business and international relations. He published *The Art of Negotiating*, where he states that the philosophies of the negotiators determine the direction a negotiation takes. His *Everybody Wins* philosophy assures that all parties benefit from the negotiation process which also produces more successful outcomes than the adversarial "winner takes all" approach.

In the 1970s, practitioners and researchers began to develop *Win-Win* approaches to negotiation. Win-Win is taken from Economic Game Theory, and has been adopted by North American negotiation academics loosely to mean Principled Negotiation. *Getting to YES* was published by Roger Fisher and William Ury as part of the Harvard negotiation project. The book's approach, referred to as Principled Negotiation, is also sometimes called *Mutual Gains Bargaining*. The mutual gains approach has been effectively applied in environmental situations as well as labour relations where the parties (e.g. management and a labour union) frame the negotiation as "problem solving". If multiple issues are discussed, differences in the parties' preferences make Win-Win negotiation possible. For example, in a labour negotiation, the union might prefer job security over wage gains. If the employers have opposite preferences, a trade is possible that is beneficial to both parties. Such a negotiation is, therefore, not an adversarial zero-sum game.

There are a tremendous number of other scholars who have contributed to the field of negotiation, including Gerard E. Watzke at Tulane University, Sara Cobb at George Mason University, Len Riskin at the University of Missouri, Howard Raiffa at Harvard, Robert McKersie and Lawrence Susskind at MIT, and Adil Najam and Jeswald Salacuse at The Fletcher School of Law and Diplomacy.

The New Creative Approach

Perhaps the most famous negotiation parable involves an argument over an orange. The most obvious approach was to simply cut it in half, each person getting a fair share. But, when the negotiators began talking to each other, exchanging information about their interests, a better solution to the problem became obvious. The person wanting the orange for juice for breakfast took that part and the person wanting the rind for making marmalade took that part. Both sides ended up with more. Neither agreement is particularly creative. The parable of the orange becomes a story about creativity when both parties decide to cooperate in planting an orange tree or even an orchard.

In a similar way, Boeing buys composite plastic wings for its new 787 Dreamliner, designed and manufactured by Japanese suppliers, and then sells the completed 787s back to Japanese airlines, all with a nice subsidy from the Japanese government. This is what is meant by creativity in negotiations.

At business schools, these days, much is being learned about creative processes. Courses are offered and dissertations proffered with "innovation" as the key buzz word at academic conferences and in corporate boardrooms. And, the more heard about innovation and creative processes, the greater is the appreciation that the Japanese approach to negotiations, by nature, uses many of the techniques commonly emphasised in any discussion of creative processes. Indeed, there appears to be a deeply fundamental explanation why the Japanese have been able to build such a successful society despite their lack of natural resources and relative isolation. While Japanese society does have its own obstacles to creativity — hierarchy and collectivism are two — they have developed a negotiation style that in many ways obviates such disadvantages. Indeed, the ten new rules for global negotiations advocated by Hernandez and Graham nicely coincide with an approach that comes naturally to the Japanese:

1. Accept only creative outcomes.
2. Understand cultures, especially your own.
3. Don't just adjust to cultural differences, exploit them.
4. Gather intelligence and reconnoitre the terrain.
5. Design the information flow and process of meetings.
6. Invest in personal relationships.
7. Persuade with questions. Seek information and understanding.
8. Make no concessions until the end.
9. Use techniques of creativity.
10. Continue creativity after negotiations.

Beyond the practices of the Japanese, credit must also be given to the luminaries in field that have long advocated creativity in negotiations.

Howard Raiffa and his colleagues recommend: '...the teams should think and plan together informally and do some joint brainstorming, which can be thought of as "dialoguing" or "prenegotiating."' The two sides make no trade-offs, commitments, or arguments about how to divide the pie at this early stage. Roger Fisher and William Ury title their Chapter 4 in *Getting to Yes,* "Inventing Options for Mutual Gain." David Lax and James Sebenius, in their important new book, *3D-Negotiations,* go past getting to yes, and talk about "creative agreements" and "great agreements." Lawrence Susskind and his associates recommend "parallel informal negotiations" towards building creative negotiation outcomes. These ideas must be pushed to the forefront in thinking about negotiations. The field generally is still stuck in the past, talking about "making deals" and "solving problems" as above. Even the use of terms like "Win-Win" expose the vestiges of the old competitive thinking. The point is that a negotiation is not something that can be won or lost, and the competitive metaphor limits creativity. The problem-solving metaphor does as well. Thus, the first rule of negotiations is: Accept only creative outcomes! Lynda Lawrence at Idea Works, a Newport Beach consulting firm has developed a most useful list of ways to generate more ideas during negotiations:

Ways to Generate More Ideas:

1. Establish common goals of what this "collaboration" would create. A more workable deal? Some common long term goals? A closer partnership?
2. *Establish the rules of engagement:* The purpose of the exercise is to resolve differences in creative ways that work better for both parties. All ideas are possibilities, and research shows that combining ideas from different cultures can result in better outcomes than those from a single culture.
3. Trust is key, and difficult to establish in many cultures. Certain techniques might speed that process a little. Being offsite, for example. Establishing physical proximity that unconsciously signals intimacy.

4. Add diversity (gender, culture, extroverts, different work specialities, experts, outsiders) to the group. Indeed, the diversity associated with international teams and alliances is the real goldmine of creativity in negotiations.
5. Use storytelling. This both helps establish who you are and what point of view you are bringing to this collaboration.
6. Work in small groups. Add physical movement. Tell the participants to relax, play, sing, have fun, and silence is OK.
7. Work holistically and using visuals. If, for example, there are three sticking points where neither side is happy, agree to work on those points by spending a short time — 10 minutes — on each point where both sides offer "crazy" suggestions. Use techniques of improvisation. Neither side should be offended by the crazy ideas. No one should criticise. Explain that by exploring crazy ideas that better ideas are often generated.
8. Sleep on it. This enables the unconscious to work on the problems, and gives negotiators time to collect opinions before meeting again the next day. Other kinds of breaks, coffee, etc. are also helpful. The overnight part is particularly important. Anthropologist and consumer expert Clotaire Rapaille suggests that the transitions between wakefulness and sleep allow new kinds of thinking "...calming their brainwaves, getting them to that tranquil point just before sleep".
9. Doing this process over several sessions allows both sides to feel that progress is being made, and actually generates better and more polished ideas that both sides can invest in.
10. It is the process of creating something together, rather than the specific proposals, which creates bonding around a shared task and establishes new ways of working together. Each side feels honoured and all can feel that something is being accomplished.

For the Japanese reader, some of these will be quite familiar. It's easy to get Japanese in close physical proximity (No.3), they've been living that way for millennia. In Japanese companies there are not so much marketing specialists as different from engineers as different from finance analysts. Each executive may have worked in several functional areas, limiting the "chimney effect" often associated disparagingly with American firms (No.4). Physical movement (No.6) — picture the start of the day at the typical Japanese factory. The Japanese also seem to work best in small groups (No.6). Silence is definitely OK (part of No.6). The Japanese invented karaoke (No.6). The Japanese have difficulty criticising others, especially foreigners (No.7). The use of visuals and holistic thinking are natural for Japanese (No.7). Breaks are also a common procedure for Japanese (No.8). Japanese will work better with people with whom they are familiar (No.9).

It should also be noted that some of these techniques will seem foreign to Japanese negotiators. For example, diversity is not a strong suit for Japanese — purposefully adding women and other elements of diversity (No.4) to their groups would seem odd. However, the two key things the Japanese do in negotiation that others can and should learn are: First, the Japanese are the absolute champion information vacuums on the planet. They keep their mouths shut and let everyone else do the talking. Thus, they use the diversity of their international colleagues (customers, suppliers, competitors, scientists, etc.) to a greater extent than any other society. Often this is denigrated as copying and borrowing, but in fact being open to everyone's ideas has always been the key to creativity and human progress. While the Japanese, like everyone else around the world, are ethnocentric, they still very much respect foreign ideas. Second, the Japanese will only work with dolphins (cooperative negotiators), that is, when they have a choice. Trust and creativity go hand-in-hand. And, they will work to train their foreign counterparts to behave more cooperatively for the latter's own good. Witness the 25 year joint venture between Toyota and General Motors for manufacturing small cars in Fremont, CA as a prominent example.

Application of principles of creativity will be appropriate in at least three points during negotiations. Above noted was Howard Raiffa's suggestion that they be used in prenegotiation meetings. Second, others advocate their use when impasses are reached. For example, in the negotiations regarding the Rio Urubamba natural gas project in Peru, the involved firms and environmentalist groups reached what at the time seemed to be an irreconcilable difference — roads and a huge pipeline through the pristine forest would be an ecological disaster. The creative solution? Think of the remote gas field as an offshore platform, run the pipeline underground, and fly in personnel and equipment as needed.

Finally, even when negotiators have arrived at "yes," a scheduled review of the agreement may actually move the relationship past "yes" to truly creative outcomes. Perhaps such a review might be scheduled six months after implementation of the agreement has begun. But, the point is, time must be set aside for a creative discussion of how to improve on the agreed to relationship.

Other Negotiation Styles

Shell identified five styles/responses to negotiation. Individuals can often have strong dispositions towards numerous styles; the style used during a negotiation depends on the context and the interests of the other party, among other factors. In addition, styles can change over time.

1. *Accommodating:* Individuals who enjoy solving the other party's problems and preserving personal relationships. Accommodators are sensitive to the emotional states, body language, and verbal signals of the other parties. They can, however, feel taken advantage of in situations when the other party places little emphasis on the relationship.
2. *Avoiding:* Individuals who do not like to negotiate and don't do it unless warranted. When negotiating, avoiders tend to defer and dodge the confrontational aspects of negotiating; however, they may be perceived as tactful and diplomatic.
3. *Collaborating:* Individuals who enjoy negotiations that involve solving tough problems in creative ways. Collaborators are good at using negotiations to understand the concerns and interests of the other parties. They can, however, create problems by transforming simple situations into more complex ones.
4. *Competing:* Individuals who enjoy negotiations because they present an opportunity to win something. Competitive negotiators have strong instincts for all aspects of negotiating and are often strategic. Because their style can dominate the bargaining process, competitive negotiators often neglect the importance of relationships.
5. *Compromising:* Individuals who are eager to close the deal by doing what is fair and equal for all parties involved in the negotiation. Compromisers can be useful when there is limited time to complete the deal; however, compromisers often

unnecessarily rush the negotiation process and make concessions too quickly.

Negotiation Tactics

1. *Bad guy/good guy:* A tactic where one negotiator acts as a bad guy by using anger and threats. The other negotiator acts as a good guy by being considerate and understanding. The good guy blames the bad guy for all the difficulties while trying to get concessions and agreement from the opponent.
2. *Omission & Errors:* This tactic is used to gain certain advantages in low trust and one time negotiations. A common omission may be not including taxes and registration fees in the price of the auto until the buyer is ready to sign.
3. *Listening:* This tactic requires concentrating on what the opponents say, making eye contact and taking notes to let them know that you are attentive to their needs. Listening can also help pick up opponents negotiation tactics.

Emotion in Negotiation

Emotions play an important part in the negotiation process, although it is only in recent years that their effect is being studied. Emotions have the potential to play either a positive or negative role in negotiation. During negotiations, the decision as to whether or not to settle, rests in part on emotional factors. Negative emotions can cause intense and even irrational behaviour, and can cause conflicts to escalate and negotiations to break down, while positive emotions facilitate reaching an agreement and help to maximise joint gains.

Affect Effect

Dispositional affects affect the various stages of the negotiation process: which strategies are planned to be used, which strategies are actually chosen, the way the other party and its intentions are perceived, the willingness to reach an agreement and the final outcomes. Positive Affectivity (PA) and Negative Affectivity (NA) of one or more of the negotiating sides can lead to very different outcomes.

Positive Effect in Negotiation

Even before the negotiation process starts, people in a positive mood have more confidence, and higher tendencies to plan to use a cooperative strategy. During the negotiation, negotiators who are in a positive mood tend to enjoy the interaction more, show less contentious behaviour, use less aggressive tactics and more cooperative strategies. This in turn increases the likelihood that parties will reach their instrumental goals, and enhance the ability to find integrative gains.

Indeed, compared with negotiators with negative or natural affectivity, negotiators with positive affectivity reached more agreements and tended to honour those agreements more. Those favourable outcomes are due to better decision-making processes, such as flexible thinking, creative problem solving, respect for others' perspectives, willingness to take risks and higher confidence. Post-negotiation positive affect has beneficial consequences as well. It increases satisfaction with achieved outcome and influences one's desire for future interactions. The PA aroused by reaching an agreement facilitates the dyadic relationship, which result in affective commitment that sets the stage for subsequent interactions.

PA also has its drawbacks: it distorts perception of self performance, such that performance is judged to be relatively better than it actually is. Thus, studies involving self reports on achieved outcomes might be biased.

Negative Effect in Negotiation

Negative affect has detrimental effects on various stages in the negotiation process. Although various negative emotions affect negotiation outcomes, by far the most researched is anger. Angry negotiators plan to use more competitive strategies and to cooperate less, even before the negotiation starts. These competitive strategies are related to reduced joint outcomes. During negotiations, anger disrupts the process by reducing the level of trust, clouding parties' judgement, narrowing parties' focus of attention and changing their central goal from reaching agreement to retaliating against the other side. Angry negotiators pay less attention to opponent's interests and are less accurate in judging their interests, thus achieve lower joint gains.

Moreover, because anger makes negotiators more self-centred in their preferences, it increases the likelihood that they will reject profitable offers. Anger doesn't help in achieving negotiation goals either: it reduces joint gains and does not help to boost personal gains, as angry negotiators don't succeed in claiming more for themselves. Moreover, negative emotions lead to acceptance of settlements that are not in the positive utility function but rather have a negative utility. However, expression of negative emotions during negotiation can sometimes be beneficial: legitimately expressed anger can be an effective way to show one's commitment, sincerity, and needs. Moreover, although NA reduces gains in integrative tasks, it is a better strategy than PA in distributive tasks (such as zero-sum).

Conditions for Emotion Effect in Negotiation

Research indicates that negotiator's emotions do not necessarily affect the negotiation process. Albarracyn *et al.* (2003) suggested that there are two conditions for emotional effect, both related to the ability (presence of environmental or cognitive disturbances) and the motivation:

1. *Identification of the affect:* Requires high motivation, high ability or both.
2. *Determination that the affect is relevant and important for the judgement:* Requires that either the motivation, the ability or both are low.

According to this model, emotions are expected to affect negotiations only when one is high and the other is low. When both ability and motivation are low the affect will not be identified, and when both are high the affect will be identify but discounted as irrelevant for judgement. A possible implication of this model is, for example, that the positive effects PA has on negotiations will be seen only when either motivation or ability are low.

The Effect of the Partner's Emotions

Most studies on emotion in negotiations focus on the effect of the negotiator's own emotions on the process. However, what the other party feels might be just as important, as group emotions are known to affect processes both at the group and the personal levels. When it comes to negotiations, trust in the other party is a necessary condition for its emotion to affect, and visibility enhances the effect. Emotions contribute to negotiation processes by signalling what one feels and thinks and can thus prevent the other party from engaging in destructive behaviours and to indicate what steps should be taken next: PA signals to keep in the same way, while NA points that mental or behavioural adjustments are needed.

Partner's emotions can have two basic effects on negotiator's emotions and behaviour: mimetic/reciprocal or complementary. For example, disappointment or sadness might lead to compassion and more cooperation. In a study by Butt *et al.* (2005) which simulated real multi-phase negotiation, most people reacted to the partner's emotions in reciprocal, rather than complementary, manner. Specific emotions were found to have different effects on the opponent's feelings and strategies chosen:

- Anger caused the opponents to place lower demands and to concede more in a zero-sum negotiation, but also to evaluate the negotiation less favourably. It provoked both dominating and yielding behaviours of the opponent.
- Pride led to more integrative and compromise strategies by the partner.
- Guilt or regret expressed by the negotiator led to better impression of him by the opponent, however, it also led the opponent to place higher demands. On the other hand, personal guilt was related to more satisfaction with what one achieved.
- Worry or disappointment left bad impression on the opponent, but led to relatively lower demands by the opponent.

Problems with Lab Negotiation Studies

Negotiation is a rather complex interaction. Capturing all its complexity is a very difficult task, let alone isolating and controlling only certain aspects of it. For this reason most negotiation studies are done under laboratory conditions, and focus only on some aspects. Although lab studies have their advantages, they do have major drawbacks when studying emotions:

- Emotions in lab studies are usually manipulated and are, therefore, relatively 'cold' (not intense). Although those 'cold' emotions might be enough to show effects, they are qualitatively different from the 'hot' emotions often experienced during negotiations.
- In real life there is self-selection to which negotiation one gets into, which effects the emotional commitment, motivation and interests. However, this is not the case in lab studies.

- Lab studies tend to focus on relatively few well defined emotions. Real life scenarios provoke a much wider scale of emotions.
- Coding the emotions has a double catch: if done by a third side, some emotions might not be detected as the negotiator sublimates them for strategic reasons. Self report measures might overcome this, but they are usually filled only before or after the process, and if filled during the process might interfere with it.

Pervasive Impact of Culture on International Negotiations

The primary purpose of this section is to demonstrate the extent of cultural differences in negotiation styles and how these differences can cause problems in international business negotiations. The reader will note that national culture does not determine negotiation behaviour. Rather, national culture is one of many factors that influence behaviour at the negotiation table, albeit an important one. For example, gender, organisational culture, international experience, industry or regional background can all be important influences as well. Of course, stereotypes of all kinds are dangerous, and international negotiators must get to know the people they are working with, not just their culture, country, or company.

The material here is based on systematic study of international negotiation behaviour over the last three decades in which the negotiation styles of more than 1,500 businesspeople in 18 countries (21 cultures) were considered. The work involved interviews with experienced executives and participant observations in the field, as well as behavioural science laboratory work including surveys and analyses of videotaped negotiations. The countries studied were Japan, S. Korea, Taiwan, China (Tianjin, Guangzhou, and Hong Kong), Vietnam, the Philippines, Russia, Israel, Norway, the Czech Republic, Germany, France, the United Kingdom, Spain, Brazil, Mexico, Canada (English-speakers and French-speakers), and the United States. The countries were chosen because they constitute America's most important present and future trading partners.

Looking broadly across the several cultures, two important lessons stand out. The first is that regional generalisations very often are not correct. For example, Japanese and Korean negotiation styles are quite similar in some ways, but in other ways they could not be more different. The second lesson learned from the research is that Japan is an exceptional place: On almost every dimension of negotiation style considered, the Japanese are on or near the end of the scale. For example, the Japanese use the lowest amount of eye contact of the cultures studied. Sometimes, Americans are on the other end. But actually, most of the time Americans are somewhere in the middle. The reader will see this evinced in the data presented in this section. The Japanese approach, however, is most distinct, even *sui generis*.

Cultural differences cause four kinds of problems in international business negotiations, at the levels of:

- Language;
- Nonverbal behaviours;
- Values; and
- Thinking and decision-making processes.

The order is important; the problems lower on the list are more serious because they are more subtle. For example, two negotiators would notice immediately if one were speaking Japanese and the other German. The solution to the problem may be as simple as hiring an interpreter or talking in a common third language, or it may be as difficult as learning a language. Regardless of the solution, the problem is obvious.

Cultural differences in non-verbal behaviours, on the other hand, are almost always hidden below our awareness. That is to say, in a face-to-face negotiation participants non-verbally—and more subtly—give off and take in a great deal of information. Some experts argue that this information is more important than verbal information. Almost all this signalling goes on below our levels of consciousness. When the non-verbal signals from foreign partners are different, negotiators are most apt to misinterpret them without even being conscious of the mistake.

For example, when a French client consistently interrupts, Americans tend to feel uncomfortable without noticing exactly why. In this manner, interpersonal friction often colours business relationships, goes undetected, and, consequently, goes uncorrected. Differences in values and thinking and decision-making processes are hidden even deeper and, therefore, are even harder to diagnose and, therefore, cure. These differences are discussed below, starting with language and non-verbal behaviours.

Differences at the Level of Language

Translation problems are often substantial in international negotiations. And, when languages are linguistically distant, greater problems should be anticipated. Particularly daunting can be work in global negotiation. Often the language used is English, but it may be spoken as a second language by most executives at the table. Indeed, native speakers from England, India, and the United States often have trouble understanding one another. Exact translations in international interactions are a goal almost never attained.

Moreover, language differences are sometimes exploited in interesting ways. Many senior executives in foreign countries speak and understand some English, but prefer to speak in their "stronger" native language and use an interpreter. Thus, we've seen a senior Russian negotiator asking questions in Russian. The interpreter then translated the question for his American counterpart. While the interpreter spoke, the American's attention (gaze direction) was given to the interpreter. However, the Russian's gaze direction was at the American. Therefore, the Russian could carefully and unobtrusively observe the American's facial expressions and non-verbal responses. Additionally, when the American spoke, the senior Russian had twice the response time. Because he understood English, he could formulate his responses during the translation process.

What's this extra response time worth in a strategic conversation? What's it worth to be carefully able to observe the non-verbal responses of your top-level counterpart in a high-stakes business negotiation? Simply stated, bilingualism is not a common characteristic for Americans, and therefore competitors with greater language skills are afforded a natural advantage in international commerce.

Additionally, a common complaint heard from American managers regards foreign clients and partners breaking into side conversations in their native languages. At best, it is seen as impolite, and quite often American negotiators are likely to attribute something sinister to the content of the foreign talk—"They're plotting or telling secrets." This is a frequent American mistake.

The usual purpose of such side conversations is to straighten out a translation problem. For instance, one Korean may lean over to another and ask, "What did he say?" Or, the side conversation can regard a disagreement among the foreign team members. Both circumstances should be seen as positive signs by Americans—that is, getting translations straight enhances the efficiency of the interactions, and concessions often follow internal disagreements. But because most Americans speak only one language, neither circumstance is appreciated. By the way, people from other countries are advised to give Americans a brief explanation of the content of their first few side conversations to assuage the sinister attributions.

But, there are problems at the level of language beyond translations and interpreters. Data from simulated negotiations are informative. In the study, the verbal behaviours of negotiators in 15 of the cultures (six negotiators in each of the 15 groups) were videotaped. The numbers in the study represent the percentages of statements that were classified into each category listed. That is, 7 per cent of the statements made by Japanese negotiators were classified as promises, 4 per cent as threats, 7 per cent as recommendations, and so on.

The verbal bargaining behaviours used by the negotiators during the simulations proved to be surprisingly similar across cultures. Negotiations in all 15 cultures were composed primarily of information-exchange tactics—questions and self-disclosures. Note that the Israelis are on the low end of the continuum of self-disclosures. Their 30 per cent (near the Japanese, Spaniards, and the English-speaking Canadians at 34 per cent) was the lowest across all 15 groups, suggesting that they are the most reticent about giving (that is, communicating) information. Overall, however, the patterns of verbal tactics used were surprisingly similar across the diverse cultures.

Nonverbal Behaviours

Anthropologist Ray L. Birdwhistell demonstrated that less than 35 per cent of the message in conversations is conveyed by the spoken word while the other 65 per cent is communicated non-verbally. Albert Mehrabian, a UCLA psychologist, also parsed where meaning comes from in face-to-face interactions. He reports:

- 7 per cent of the meaning is derived from the words spoken;
- 38 per cent from paralinguistic channels, that is, tone of voice, loudness, and other aspects of how things are said; and
- 55 per cent from facial expressions.

Of course, some might quibble with the exact percentages (and many have), but our work also supports the notion that non-verbal behaviours are crucial — how things are said is often more important than what is said.

The study provides analyses of some linguistic aspects and non-verbal behaviours for the 15 videotaped groups, that is, how things are said. Although these efforts merely scratch the surface of these kinds of behavioural analyses, they still provide indications of substantial cultural differences. Note that, once again, the Japanese are at or next to the end of the continuum on almost every dimension of the behaviours listed. Their facial gazing and touching are the least among the 15 groups. Only the Northern Chinese used the word no less frequently, and only the Russians used more silent periods than did the Japanese.

A broader examination of the data in the study reveals a more meaningful conclusion: The variation across cultures is greater when comparing linguistic aspects of language and non-verbal behaviours than when the verbal content of negotiations is considered.

Distinctive Negotiation Behaviours of 15 Cultural Groups

Following are further descriptions of the distinctive aspects of each of the 15 cultural groups videotaped. Certainly, conclusions of statistical significant differences between individual cultures cannot be drawn without larger sample sizes. But, the suggested cultural differences are worthwhile to consider briefly.

Japan: Consistent with most descriptions of Japanese negotiation behaviour, the results of this analysis suggest their style of interaction is among the least aggressive (or most polite). Threats, commands, and warnings appear to be de-emphasised in favour of the more positive promises, recommendations, and commitments. Particularly indicative of their polite conversational style was their infrequent use of *no* and *you* and facial gazing, as well as more frequent silent periods.

Korea: Perhaps one of the more interesting aspects of the analysis is the contrast of the Asian styles of negotiations. Non-Asians often generalise about the Orient; the findings demonstrate, however, that this is a mistake. Korean negotiators used considerably more punishments and commands than did the Japanese. Koreans used the word no and interrupted more than three times as frequently as the Japanese. Moreover, no silent periods occurred between Korean negotiators.

China (Northern): The behaviours of the negotiators from Northern China (i.e., in and around Tianjin) were most remarkable in the emphasis on asking questions (34%). Indeed, 70 per cent of the statements made by the Chinese negotiators were classified as information-exchange tactics. Other aspects of their behaviour were quite similar to the Japanese, particularly the use of *no* and *you* and silent periods.

Taiwan: The behaviour of the businesspeople in Taiwan was quite different from that in China and Japan but similar to that in Korea. The Chinese on Taiwan were exceptional in the time of facial gazing—on the average, almost 20 of 30 minutes. They asked fewer questions and provided more information (self-disclosures) than did any of the other Asian groups.

Russia: The Russians' style was quite different from that of any other European group, and, indeed, was quite similar in many respects to the style of the Japanese. They used *no* and *you* infrequently and used the most silent periods of any group. Only the Japanese did less facial gazing, and only the Chinese asked a greater percentage of questions.

Israel: The behaviours of the Israeli negotiators were distinctive in three respects. As mentioned above, they used the lowest percentage of self-disclosures, apparently holding their cards relatively closely. Alternatively, they used by far the highest percentages of promises and recommendations, using these persuasive strategies unusually heavily. They were also at the end of the scale on the percentage of normative appeals at 5 per cent with the most frequent reference to competitors' offers. Perhaps most importantly the Israeli negotiators interrupted one another much more frequently than negotiators from any other group. Indeed, this important non-verbal behaviour is most likely to blame for the "pushy" stereotype often used by Americans to describe their Israeli negotiation partners.

Germany: The behaviours of the Germans are difficult to characterise because they fell towards the centre of almost all the continua. However, the Germans were exceptional in the high percentage of self-disclosures (47%) and the low percentage of questions (11%).

United Kingdom: The behaviours of the British negotiators were remarkably similar to those of the Americans in all respects.

Spain: *Diga* is perhaps a good metaphor for the Spanish approach to negotiations evinced in our data. When you make a phone call in Madrid, the usual greeting on the other end is not *hola* (hello) but is, instead, *diga* (speak). It is not surprising, then, that the Spaniards in the videotaped negotiations likewise used the highest percentage of commands (17%) of any of the groups and gave comparatively little information (self-disclosures, only 34 per cent). Moreover, they interrupted one another more frequently than any other group, and they used the terms *no* and *you* very frequently.

France: The style of the French negotiators was perhaps the most aggressive of all the groups. In particular, they used the highest percentage of threats and warnings (together, 8 per cent). They also used interruptions, facial gazing, and *no* and *you* very frequently compared with the other groups, and one of the French negotiators touched his partner on the arm during the simulation.

Brazil: The Brazilian businesspeople, like the French and Spanish, were quite aggressive. They used the second-highest percentage of commands of all the groups. On average, the Brazilians said the word *no* 42 times, *you* 90 times, and touched one another on the arm about 5 times during 30 minutes of negotiation. Facial gazing was also high.

Mexico: The patterns of Mexican behaviour in our negotiations are good reminders of the dangers of regional or language-group generalisations. Both verbal and non-verbal behaviours were quite different than those of their Latin American (Brazilian) or continental (Spanish) cousins. Indeed, Mexicans answer the telephone with the much less demanding *bueno* (short for "good day"). In many respects, the Mexican behaviour was very similar to that of the negotiators from the United States.

French-Speaking Canada: The French-speaking Canadians behaved quite similarly to their continental cousins. Like the negotiators from France, they too used high percentages of threats and warnings, and even more interruptions and eye contact. Such an aggressive interaction style would not mix well with some of the more low-key styles of some of the Asian groups or with English speakers, including English-speaking Canadians.

English-Speaking Canada: The Canadians who speak English as their first language used the lowest percentage of aggressive persuasive tactics (threats, warnings, and punishments totalled only 1 per cent) of all 15 groups. Perhaps, as communications researchers suggest, such stylistic differences are the seeds of interethnic discord as witnessed in Canada over the years. With respect to international negotiations, the English-speaking Canadians used noticeably more interruptions and *no's* than negotiators from either of Canada's major trading partners, the United States and Japan.

United States: Like the Germans and the British, the Americans fell in the middle of most continua. They did interrupt one another less frequently than all the others, but that was their sole distinction.

These differences across the cultures are quite complex, and this material by itself should not be used to predict the behaviours of foreign counterparts. Instead, great care should be taken with respect to the aforementioned dangers of stereotypes. The key here is to be aware of these kinds of differences so that the Japanese silence, the Brazilian "no, no, no...," or the French threat are not misinterpreted.

3

Negotiation Theory

The foundations of negotiation theory are decision analysis, behavioural decision-making, game theory, and negotiation analysis. Another classification of theories distinguishes between Structural Analysis, Strategic Analysis, Process Analysis, Integrative Analysis and Behavioural Analysis of negotiations.

Individuals should make separate, interactive decisions; and *negotiation analysis* considers how groups of reasonably bright individuals should and could make joint, collaborative decisions. These theories are interleaved and should be approached from the synthetic perspective.

Common Assumptions of Most Theories

Negotiation is a specialised and formal version of conflict resolution most frequently employed when important issues must be agreed upon. Negotiation is necessary when one party requires the other party's agreement to achieve its aim. The aim of negotiating is to build a shared environment leading to long-term trust and often involves a third, neutral party to extract the issues from the emotions and keep the individuals concerned focused. It is a powerful method for resolving conflict and requires skill and experience. Zartman defines negotiation as "a process of combining conflicting positions into a common position under a decision rule of unanimity, a phenomenon in which the outcome is determined by the process."

However, most theories of negotiations share the notion of negotiations as a process. Yet, they differ in their description of the process. Structural Analysis considers this process to be a power game. Strategic Analysis thinks of it as a repetition of games (Game Theory). Integrative Analysis prefers the more intuitive notion of process, in which negotiations undergo successive stages, e.g. prenegotiation, stalemate, settlement.

Especially structural, strategic and procedural analysis build on rational actors, who are able to prioritise clear goals, are able to make trade-offs between conflicting values, are consistent in their behavioural pattern, and are able to take uncertainty into account.

Negotiations differ from mere coercion, in that negotiating parties have the theoretic possibility to withdraw from negotiations. It is easier to study bilateral negotiations, as opposed to multilateral negotiations.

Structural Analysis

Structural Analysis is based on a distribution of empowering elements among two negotiating parties. Structural theory moves away from traditional Realist notions of power in that it does not only consider power to be a possession, manifested for example in economic or military resources, but also thinks of power as a relation.

Based on the distribution of elements, in structural analysis we find either power-symmetry between equally strong parties or power-asymmetry between a stronger and a weaker party. All elements from which the respective parties can draw power constitute structure. They may be of material nature, i.e. hard power, (such as weapons) or of social nature, i.e. soft power, (such as norms, contracts or precedents).

These instrumental elements of power, are either defined as parties' relative position (resources position) or as their relative ability to make their options prevail.

Structural Analysis is easy to criticise, because it predicts that the strongest will always win. This, however, does not always hold true.

Strategic Analysis

According to Structural Analysis, negotiations can, therefore, be described with matrices, such as the Prisoner's Dilemma, a concept taken from Game Theory. Another common game is the Chicken Dilemma.

Strategic Analysis starts with the assumption that both parties have a veto. Thus, in essence, negotiating parties can cooperate (C) or defect (D). Structural analysis then evaluates possible outcomes of negotiations (C, C; C, D; D, D; D, C), by assigning values to each of the possible outcomes. Often, cooperation of both sides yields the best outcome. The basic problem however is, that the parties can never be sure that the other is going to cooperate, mainly because of two reasons: first, decisions are made at the same time or, second, concessions of one side might not be returned. Therefore, the parties have contradicting incentives to cooperate or defect. If one party cooperates or makes a concession and the other does not, the defecting party might relatively gain more.

Trust may be built only in repetitive games through the emergence of reliable patterns of behaviour such as tit-for-tat.

Process Analysis

Process Analysis is the theory closest to haggling. Parties start from two points and converge through a series of concessions. As in Strategic Analysis, both sides have a veto (e.g. sell, not sell; pay, not pay). Process analysis also features structural assumptions, because one side may be weaker or stronger (e.g. more eager to sell, not willing to pay a certain price). Process Analysis focuses on the study of the dynamics of processes. E.g. both Zeuthen and Cross tried to find a formula in order to predict the behaviour of the other party in finding a rate of concession, in order to predict the likely outcome.

The process of negotiation, therefore, is considered to unfold between fixed points: starting point of discord, end point of convergence. The so-called security point, that is the result of optional withdrawal, is also taken into account.

Integrative Analysis

Integrative Analysis divides the process into successive stages, rather than talking about fixed points. It extends analysis to prenegotiations stages, in which parties make first contacts. The outcome is explained as the performance of the actors at different stages. Stages may include prenegotiations, finding a formula of distribution, crest behaviour, settlement.

Prisoner's Dilemma

The Prisoner's Dilemma constitutes a problem in game theory. It was originally framed by Merrill Flood and Melvin Dresher working at RAND in 1950. Albert W. Tucker formalised the game with prison sentence pay-offs and gave it the "Prisoner's Dilemma" name (Poundstone, 1992).

In its classical form, the prisoner's dilemma (*PD*) is presented as follows:

Two suspects are arrested by the police. The police have insufficient evidence for a conviction, and, having separated both prisoners, visit each of them to offer the same deal. If one testifies (defects) for the prosecution against the other and the other remains silent, the betrayer goes free and the silent accomplice receives the full 10-year sentence. If both remain silent, both prisoners are sentenced to only six months in jail for a minor charge. If each betrays the other, each receives a five-year sentence. Each prisoner must choose to betray the other or to remain silent. Each one is assured that the other would not know about the betrayal before the end of the investigation. How should the prisoners act?

If we assume that each player prefers shorter sentences to longer ones, and that each gets no utility out of lowering the other player's sentence, and that there are no reputation effects from a player's decision, then the Prisoner's Dilemma forms a non-zero-sum game in which two players may each cooperate with or defect from (i.e., betray) the other player. In this game, as in all game theory, the only concern of each individual player (prisoner) is maximising his/her own pay-off, without any concern for the other player's pay-off. The unique equilibrium for this game is a Pareto-suboptimal solution—that is, rational choice leads the two players to both play *defect* even though each player's individual reward would be greater if they both played *cooperatively*.

In the classic form of this game, cooperating is strictly dominated by defecting, so that the only possible equilibrium for the game is for all players to defect. No matter what the other player does, one player will always gain a greater pay-off by playing defect. Since in any situation playing *defect* is more beneficial than cooperating, all rational players will play *defect*, all things being equal.

In the iterated Prisoner's Dilemma the game is played repeatedly. Thus, each player has an opportunity to punish the other player for previous non-cooperative play. If the number of steps is known by both players in advance, economic theory says that the two players should defect again and again, no matter how many times the game is played. Only when the players play an indefinite or random number of times can cooperation be an economic equilibrium. In this case, the incentive to defect can be overcome by the threat of punishment. When the game is infinitely repeated, cooperation may be a subgame, Perfect Nash equilibrium, although both players defecting always remains an equilibrium and there are many other equilibrium outcomes. In casual usage, the label "Prisoner's Dilemma" may be applied to situations not strictly matching the formal criteria of the classic or iterative games; for instance, those in which two entities could gain important benefits from cooperating or suffer from the failure to do so, but find it merely difficult or expensive, not necessarily impossible, to coordinate their activities to achieve cooperation.

Strategy for the Classical Prisoner's Dilemma

The Classical Prisoner's Dilemma can be summarised thus:

	Prisoner B Stays Silent	*Prisoner B Betrays*
Prisoner A Stays Silent	Each serves 6 months	Prisoner A: 10 years Prisoner B: goes free
Prisoner A Betrays	Prisoner A: goes free Prisoner B: 10 years	Each serves 5 years

In this game, regardless of what the opponent chooses, each player always receives a higher pay-off (lesser sentence) by betraying; that is to say that betraying is the *strictly dominant strategy*. For instance, Prisoner A can accurately say, "*No matter what Prisoner B does,* I personally am better off betraying than staying silent. Therefore, for my own sake, I should betray." However, if the other player acts similarly, then they both betray and both get a lower pay-off than they would get by staying silent.

Rational self-interested decisions result in each prisoner's being worse off than if each chose to lessen the sentence of the accomplice at the cost of staying a little longer in jail himself (hence the seeming dilemma). In game theory, this demonstrates very elegantly that in a non-zero sum game a Nash Equilibrium need not be a Pareto optimum.

Generalised Form

We can expose the skeleton of the game by stripping it off the prisoner framing device. The generalised form of the game has been used frequently in experimental economics. The following rules give a typical realisation of the game. There are two players and a banker. Each player holds a set of two cards: one printed with the word "Cooperate", the other printed with "Defect" (the standard terminology for the game). Each player puts one card face-down in front of the banker. By laying them face down, the possibility of a player knowing the other player's selection in advance is eliminated (although revealing one's move does not affect the dominance analysis). At the end of the turn, the banker turns over both cards and gives out the payments accordingly.

If player 1 (red) defects and player 2 (blue) cooperates, player 1 gets the Temptation to Defect pay-off of 5 points while player 2 receives the Sucker's pay-off of 0 points. If both cooperate they get the Reward for Mutual Cooperation pay-off of 3 points each, while if they both defect they get the Punishment for Mutual Defection pay-off of 1 point. The checker board pay-off matrix showing the pay-offs is given below.

Example PD pay-off matrix

	Cooperate	*Defect*
Cooperate	3, 3	0, 5
Defect	5, 0	1, 1

In "win-lose" terminology the table looks like this:

	Cooperate	*Defect*
Cooperate	win-win	lose much-win much
Defect	win much-lose much	lose-lose

These point assignments are given arbitrarily for illustration. It is possible to generalise them, as follows:

Canonical PD pay-off matrix

	Cooperate	*Defect*
Cooperate	R, R	S, T
Defect	T, S	P, P

Where *T* stands for *Temptation to defect*, *R* for *Reward for mutual cooperation*, *P* for *Punishment for mutual defection* and *S* for *Sucker's pay-off*. To be defined as Prisoner's Dilemma, the following inequalities must hold:

$$T > R > P > S$$

This condition ensures that the equilibrium outcome is defection, but that cooperation Pareto dominates equilibrium play. In addition to the above condition, if the game is repeatedly played by two players, the following condition should be added.

$$2R > T + S$$

If that condition does not hold, then full cooperation is not necessarily Pareto optimal, as the players are collectively better off by having each player alternate between Cooperate and Defect.

These rules were established by cognitive scientist Douglas Hofstadter and form the formal canonical description of a typical game of Prisoner's Dilemma.

A simple special case occurs when the advantage of defection over cooperation is independent of what the coplayer does and cost of the coplayers defection is independent of one's own action, i.e. $T + S = P + R$.

Human Behaviour in Prisoner's Dilemma

One experiment based on the simple dilemma found that approximately 40 per cent of participants played "cooperate" (i.e., stayed silent).

Iterated Prisoner's Dilemma

If two players play Prisoner's Dilemma more than once in succession and they remember previous actions of their opponent and change their strategy accordingly, the game is called *iterated Prisoner's Dilemma*. If the game is played exactly N times, the dominant strategy is for both players to defect N times.

The proof is by induction: assume the players play N+1 times. On the last step, there is no possibility of punishment, so the two rational players defect. But then the game is reduced to the N step dilemma, and the induction is complete.

Unlike the standard Prisoner's Dilemma, in the iterated Prisoner's Dilemma the defection strategy is counterintuitive and fails badly to predict the behaviour of human players. Within standard economic theory, though, this is the only correct answer.

If the number N is not known by the players ahead of time, and if the probability of the two players playing another game is sufficiently large, cooperation can be the stable strategy within standard economic theory. Amongst results shown by Nobel Prize winner Robert Aumann in his 1959 paper, rational players repeatedly interacting for indefinitely long games can sustain the cooperative outcome. Interest in the iterated Prisoner's Dilemma (IPD) was kindled by Robert Axelrod in his book *The Evolution of Cooperation* (1984). In this he reports on a tournament he organised of the N step Prisoner's Dilemma (with N fixed) in which participants have to choose their mutual strategy again and again, and have memory of their previous encounters. Axelrod invited academic colleagues all over the world to devise computer strategies to compete in an IPD tournament. The programmes that were entered varied widely in algorithmic complexity, initial hostility, capacity for forgiveness, and so forth.

Axelrod discovered that when these encounters were repeated over a long period of time with many players, each with different strategies, greedy strategies tended to do very poorly in the long run while more altruistic strategies did better, as judged purely by self-interest. He used this to show a possible mechanism for the evolution of altruistic behaviour from mechanisms that are initially purely selfish, by natural selection.

The best deterministic strategy was found to be "Tit for Tat," which Anatol Rapoport developed and entered into the tournament. It was the simplest of any programme entered, containing only four lines of BASIC, and won the contest. The strategy is simply to cooperate on the first iteration of the game; after that, the player does what his opponent did on the previous move. Depending on the situation, a slightly better strategy can be "Tit for Tat with forgiveness." When the opponent defects, on the next move, the player sometimes cooperates anyway, with a small probability (around 1-5%). This allows for occasional recovery from getting trapped in a cycle of defections. The exact probability depends on the line-up of opponents.

By analysing the top-scoring strategies, Axelrod stated several conditions necessary for a strategy to be successful.

Nice: The most important condition is that the strategy must be "nice", that is, it will not defect before its opponent does (this is sometimes referred to as an "optimistic" algorithm). Almost all of the top-scoring strategies were nice; therefore a purely selfish strategy will not "cheat" on its opponent, for purely utilitarian reasons first.

Retaliating: However, Axelrod contended, the successful strategy must not be a blind optimist. It must sometimes retaliate. An example of a non-retaliating strategy is Always Cooperate. This is a very bad choice, as "nasty" strategies will ruthlessly exploit such players.

Forgiving: Successful strategies must also be forgiving. Though players will retaliate, they will once again fall back to cooperating if the opponent does not continue to defect. This stops long runs of revenge and counter-revenge, maximising points.

Non-envious: The last quality is being non-envious, that is not striving to score more than the opponent (impossible for a 'nice' strategy, i.e., a 'nice' strategy can never score more than the opponent).

Therefore, Axelrod reached the oxymoron-sounding conclusion that selfish individuals for their own selfish good will tend to be nice and forgiving and non-envious.

The optimal (points-maximising) strategy for the one-time PD game is simply defection; as explained above, this is true whatever the composition of opponents may be. However, in the iterated-PD game the optimal strategy depends upon the strategies of likely opponents, and how they will react to defections and cooperations. For example, consider a population where everyone defects every time, except for a single individual following the Tit-for-Tat strategy. That individual is at a slight disadvantage because of the loss on the first turn. In such a population, the optimal strategy for that individual is to defect every time. In a population with a certain percentage of always-defectors and the rest being Tit-for-Tat players, the optimal strategy for an individual depends on the percentage, and on the length of the game.

A strategy called *Pavlov* (an example of Win-Stay, Lose-Switch) cooperates at the first iteration and whenever the player and coplayer did the same thing at the previous iteration; Pavlov defects when the player and coplayer did different things at the previous iteration. For a certain range of parameters, Pavlov beats all other strategies by giving preferential treatment to coplayers which resemble Pavlov.

Deriving the optimal strategy is generally done in two ways:

1. Bayesian Nash Equilibrium: If the statistical distribution of opposing strategies can be determined (e.g. 50 per cent tit-for-tat, 50 per cent always cooperate) an optimal counter-strategy can be derived analytically.
2. Monte Carlo simulations of populations have been made, where individuals with low scores die off, and those with high scores reproduce (a genetic algorithm for finding an optimal strategy). The mix of algorithms in the final population generally depends on the mix in the initial population. The introduction of mutation (random variation during reproduction) lessens the dependency on the initial population; empirical experiments with such systems tend to produce Tit-for-Tat players, but there is no analytic proof that this will always occur.

Although Tit-for-Tat is considered to be the most robust basic strategy, a team from Southampton University in England (led by Professor Nicholas Jennings and consisting of Rajdeep Dash, Sarvapali Ramchurn, Alex Rogers, Perukrishnen Vytelingum) introduced a new strategy at the 20th-anniversary Iterated Prisoner's Dilemma competition, which proved to be more successful than Tit-for-Tat. This strategy relied on cooperation between programmes to achieve the highest number of points for a single programme. The University submitted 60 programmes to the competition, which were designed to recognise each other through a series of five to ten moves at the start. Once this recognition was made, one programme would always cooperate and the other would always defect, assuring the maximum number of points for the defector. If the programme realised that it was playing a non-Southampton player, it would continuously defect in an attempt to minimise the score of the competing programme. As a result, this strategy ended up taking the top three positions in the competition, as well as a number of positions towards the bottom.

This strategy takes advantage of the fact that multiple entries were allowed in this particular competition, and that the performance of a team was measured by that of the highest-scoring player (meaning that the use of self-sacrificing players was a form of minmaxing). In a competition where one has control of only a single player, Tit-for-Tat is certainly a better strategy. Because of this new rule, this competition also has little theoretical significance when analysing single agent strategies as compared to Axelrod's seminal tournament. However, it provided the framework for analysing how to achieve cooperative strategies in multi-agent frameworks, especially in the presence of noise. In fact, long before this new-rules tournament was played, Richard Dawkins in his book *The Selfish Gene* pointed out the possibility of such strategies winning if multiple entries were allowed, but remarked that most probably Axelrod would not have allowed them if they had been submitted. It also relies on circumventing rules about the prisoner's dilemma in that there is no communication allowed between the two players. When the Southampton programmes engage in an opening "ten move dance" to recognise one another, this only reinforces just how valuable communication can be in shifting the balance of the game.

If an iterated PD is going to be iterated exactly N times, for some known constant N, then it is always game theoretically optimal to defect in all rounds. The only possible Nash equilibrium is to always defect. The proof goes like this: one might as well defect on the last turn, since the opponent will not have a chance to punish the player. Therefore, both will defect on the last turn. Thus, the player might as well defect on the second-to-last turn, since the opponent will defect on the last no matter what is done, and so on. For cooperation to emerge between game theoretic rational players, the total number of rounds must be random, or at least unknown to the players. However, even in this case always defect is no longer a strictly dominant strategy, only a Nash equilibrium. The superrational strategy in this case is to cooperate against a superrational opponent, and in the limit of large fixed N, experimental results on strategies agree with the superrational version, not the game-theoretic rational one.

Another odd case is "play forever" Prisoner's Dilemma. The game is repeated infinitely many times and the player's score is the average (suitably computed).

The Prisoner's Dilemma game is fundamental to certain theories of human cooperation and trust. On the assumption that the PD can model transactions between two people requiring trust, cooperative behaviour in populations may be modelled by a multi-player, iterated, version of the game. It has, consequently, fascinated many scholars over the years. In 1975, Grofman and Pool estimated the count of scholarly articles devoted to it at over 2,000. The iterated Prisoner's Dilemma has also been referred to as the "Peace-War game".

Continuous Iterated Prisoner's Dilemma

Most work on the Iterated Prisoner's Dilemma has focused on the discrete case, in which players either cooperate or defect, because this model is relatively simple to analyse. However, some researchers have looked at models of the continuous Iterated Prisoner's Dilemma, in which players are able to make a variable contribution to the other player. Le and Boyd found that in such situations, cooperation is much harder to evolve than in the discrete Iterated Prisoner's Dilemma. The basic intuition for this result is straightforward: in a continuous Prisoner's Dilemma, if a population starts off in a non-cooperative equilibrium, players who are only marginally more cooperative than non-cooperators get little benefit from assorting with one another. By contrast, in a discrete prisoner's dilemma, Tit-for-Tat cooperators get a big pay-off boost from assorting with one another in a non-cooperative equilibrium, relative to non-cooperators. Since nature arguably offers more opportunities for variable cooperation rather than a strict dichotomy of cooperation or defection, the continuous prisoner's dilemma may help explain why real-life examples of Tit-for-Tat-like cooperation are extremely rare in nature (ex. Hammerstein) even though Tit-for-Tat seems robust in theoretical models.

Learning Psychology and Game Theory

Where game players can learn to estimate the likelihood of other players defecting, their own behaviour is influenced by their experience of the others' behaviour. Simple statistics show that inexperienced players are more likely to have had, overall, atypically good or bad interactions with other players. If they act on the basis of these experiences (by defecting or cooperating more than they would otherwise) they are likely to suffer in future transactions. As more experience is accrued a truer impression of the likelihood of defection is gained and game playing becomes more successful. The early transactions experienced by immature players are likely to have a greater effect on their future playing than would such transactions affect mature players. This principle goes part way towards explaining why the formative experiences of young people are so influential and why, for example, those who are particularly vulnerable to bullying sometimes become bullies themselves.

The likelihood of defection in a population may be reduced by the experience of cooperation in earlier games allowing trust to build up. Hence self-sacrificing behaviour may, in some instances, strengthen the moral fibre of a group. If the group is small the positive behaviour is more likely to feed back in a mutually affirming way, encouraging individuals within that group to continue to cooperate. This is allied to the twin dilemma of encouraging those people whom one would aid to indulge in behaviour that might put them at risk. Such processes are major concerns within the study of reciprocal altruism, group selection, kin selection and moral philosophy.

Douglas Hofstadter's Superrationality

Douglas Hofstadter in his *Metamagical Themas* proposed that the conception of rationality that led "rational" players to defect is faulty. He proposed that there is another type of rational behaviour, which he called "superrational", where players take into account that the other person is presumably superrational, like them. Superrational players behave identically and know that they will behave identically. They take that into account *before* they maximise their pay-offs, and they, therefore, cooperate with each other.

This view of the one-shot PD leads to cooperation as follows:

- any superrational strategy will be the same for both superrational players, since both players will think of it.
- therefore the superrational answer will lie on the diagonal of the pay-off matrix.
- when you maximise return from solutions on the diagonal, you cooperate.

If a superrational player plays against a known rational opponent, she will defect. A superrational player only cooperates with other superrational players, whose thinking is correlated with hers. If a superrational player plays against an opponent of unknown superrationality in a symmetric situation, the result can be either to cooperate or to defect depending on the odds that the opponent is superrational.

Superrationality is not studied by academic economists, because the economic definition of rationality excludes any superrational behaviour by definition. Nevertheless, analogs of one-shot cooperation are observed in human culture, wherever religious or ethical codes exist. Hofstadter discusses the example of an economic transaction between strangers passing through a town—where either party stands to gain by cheating the other, with little hope of retaliation. Still, cheating is the exception rather than the rule.

4

Decision Making

Decision-making can be regarded as an outcome of mental processes (cognitive process) leading to the selection of a course of action among several alternatives. Every decision-making process produces a final choice. The output can be an action or an opinion of choice.

Human performance in decision-making terms has been the subject of active research from several perspectives. From a psychological perspective, it is necessary to examine individual decisions in the context of a set of needs, preferences an individual has and values they seek. From a cognitive perspective, the decision-making process must be regarded as a continuous process integrated in the interaction with the environment. From a normative perspective, the analysis of individual decisions is concerned with the logic of decision-making and rationality and the invariant choice it leads to.

Yet, at another level, it might be regarded as a problem solving activity which is terminated when a satisfactory solution is found. Therefore, decision-making is a reasoning or emotional process which can be rational or irrational, can be based on explicit assumptions or tacit assumptions.

Logical decision-making is an important part of all science-based professions, where specialists apply their knowledge in a given area to making informed decisions. For example, medical decision-making often involves making a diagnosis and selecting an appropriate treatment. Some research using naturalistic methods shows, however, that in situations with higher time pressure, higher stakes, or increased ambiguities, experts use intuitive decision-making rather than structured approaches, following a recognition primed decision approach to fit a set of indicators into the expert's experience and immediately arrive at a satisfactory course of action without weighing alternatives.

Recent robust decision efforts have formally integrated uncertainty into the decision-making process. However, Decision Analysis, recognised and included uncertainties with a structured and rationally justifiable method of decision-making since its conception in 1964.

Decision Making Processes Topics

According to behaviouralist Isabel Briggs Myers, a person's decision-making process depends on a significant degree on their cognitive style. Myers developed a set of four bi-polar dimensions, called the *Myers-Briggs Type Indicator* (MBTI). The terminal points on these dimensions are: *thinking* and *feeling*; *extroversion* and *introversion*; *judgement* and *perception*; and *sensing* and *intuition*. She claimed that a person's decision-making style is based largely on how they score on these four dimensions. For example, someone who scored near the thinking, extroversion, sensing, and judgement ends of the dimensions would tend to have a logical, analytical, objective, critical, and empirical decision-making style.

Other studies suggest that these national or cross-cultural differences exist across entire societies. For example, Maris Martinsons has found that American, Japanese and Chinese business leaders each exhibit a distinctive national style of decision-making.

Some of the decision-making techniques that we use in everyday life include:

- listing the advantages and disadvantages of each option, popularised by Plato and Benjamin Franklin;
- flipping a coin, cutting a deck of playing cards, and other random or coincidence methods;
- accepting the first option that seems like it might achieve the desired result;

- prayer, tarot cards, astrology, augurs, revelation, or other forms of divination;
- acquiesce to a person in authority or an "expert"; and
- choosing the alternative with the highest probability-weighted utility for each alternative.

Cognitive and Personal Biases

Biases can creep into our decision-making processes. Many different people have made a decision about the same question (*e.g.* "Should I have a doctor look at this troubling breast cancer symptom I've discovered?" "Why did I ignore the evidence that the project was going over budget?") and then craft potential cognitive interventions aimed at improving decision-making outcomes.

Below is a list of some of the more commonly debated cognitive biases:

- *Selective search for evidence (a.k.a. Confirmation bias in psychology) (Scott Plous, 1993):* We tend to be willing to gather facts that support certain conclusions but disregard other facts that support different conclusions.
- *Premature termination of search for evidence:* We tend to accept the first alternative that looks like it might work.
- *Inertia:* Unwillingness to change thought patterns that we have used in the past in the face of new circumstances.
- *Selective perception:* We actively screen-out information that we do not think is salient.
- *Wishful thinking or optimism bias:* We tend to want to see things in a positive light and this can distort our perception and thinking.
- Choice-supportive bias occurs when we distort our memories of chosen and rejected options to make the chosen options seem relatively more attractive.
- *Recency:* We tend to place more attention on more recent information and either ignore or forget more distant information. The opposite effect in the first set of data or other information is termed Primacy effect (Plous, 1993).

- *Repetition bias:* A willingness to believe what we have been told most often and by the greatest number of different of sources.
- *Anchoring and adjustment:* Decisions are unduly influenced by initial information that shapes our view of subsequent information.
- *Group think:* Peer pressure to conform to the opinions held by the group.
- *Source credibility bias:* We reject something if we have a bias against the person, organisation, or group to which the person belongs: We are inclined to accept a statement by someone we like.
- *Incremental decision-making and escalating commitment:* We look at a decision as a small step in a process and this tends to perpetuate a series of similar decisions. This can be contrasted with zero-based decision-making.
- *Attribution asymmetry:* We tend to attribute our success to our abilities and talents, but we attribute our failures to bad luck and external factors. We attribute other's success to good luck, and their failures to their mistakes.
- *Role fulfilment (Self Fulfilling Prophecy):* We conform to the decision-making expectations that others have of someone in our position.
- *Underestimating uncertainty and the illusion of control:* We tend to underestimate future uncertainty because we tend to believe we have more control over events than we really do. We believe we have control to minimise potential problems in our decisions.

Neuroscience Perspective

The Anterior Cingulate Cortex (ACC), orbitofrontal cortex (and the overlapping ventromedial prefrontal cortex) are brain regions involved in decision-making processes. A recent neuroimaging study, found distinctive patterns of neural activation in these regions depending on whether decisions were made on the basis of personal volition or following directions from someone else. Patients with damage to the ventromedial prefrontal cortex have difficulty making decisions. Another recent study found that lesions to the ACC in the macaque resulted in impaired decision-making in the long run of reinforcement guided tasks suggesting that the ACC is responsible for evaluating past reinforcement information and guiding future action.

Emotion appears to aid the decision-making process: Decision-making often occurs in the face of uncertainty about whether one's choices will lead to benefit or harm. The somatic-marker hypothesis is a neurobiological theory of how decisions are made in the face of uncertain outcome. This theory holds that such decisions are aided by emotions, in the form of bodily states, that are elicited during the deliberation of future consequences and that mark different options for behaviour as being advantageous or disadvantageous. This process involves an interplay between neural systems that elicit emotional/bodily states and neural systems that map these emotional/bodily states.

Styles and Methods of Decision Making

Styles and methods of decision-making were elaborated by the founder of *Predispositioning Theory*, Aron Katsenelinboigen. In his analysis on styles and methods Katsenelinboigen referred to the game of chess, saying that "chess does disclose various methods of operation, notably the creation of predisposition—methods which may be applicable to other, more complex systems."

In his book Katsenelinboigen states that apart from the methods (reactive and selective) and sub-methods (randomisation, predispositioning, programming), there are two major styles — positional and combinational. Both styles are utilised in the game of chess. According to Katsenelinboigen, the two styles reflect two basic approaches to the uncertainty: deterministic (combinational style) and indeterministic (positional style). Katsenelinboigen's definition of the two styles are the following.

The combinational style is characterised by

- a very narrow, clearly defined, primarily material goal, and
- a programme that links the initial position with the final outcome.

In defining the combinational style in chess, Katsenelinboigen writes:

"The combinational style features a clearly formulated limited objective, namely the capture of material (the main constituent element of a chess position). The objective is implemented via a well defined and in some cases in a unique sequence of moves aimed at reaching the set goal. As a rule, this sequence leaves no options for the opponent. Finding a combinational objective allows the player to focus all his energies on efficient execution, that is, the player's analysis may be limited to the pieces directly partaking in the combination. This approach is the crux of the combination and the combinational style of play.

The positional style is distinguished by:

- a positional goal; and
- a formation of semi-complete linkages between the initial step and final outcome.

"Unlike the combinational player, the positional player is occupied, first and foremost, with the elaboration of the position that will allow him to develop in the unknown future. In playing the positional style, the player must evaluate relational and material parameters as independent variables. (...) The positional style gives the player the opportunity to develop a position until it becomes pregnant with a combination. However, the combination is not the final goal of the positional player—it helps him to achieve the desirable, keeping in mind a predisposition for the future development. The Pyrrhic victory is the best example of one's inability to think positionally."

The positional style serves to:

a. create a predisposition to the future development of the position;
b. induce the environment in a certain way;
c. absorb an unexpected outcome in one's favour; and
d. avoid the negative aspects of unexpected outcomes.

The positional style gives the player the opportunity to develop a position until it becomes pregnant with a combination. Katsenelinboigen writes:

"As the game progressed and defence became more sophisticated the combinational style of play declined.... The positional style of chess does not eliminate the combinational one with its attempt to see the entire programme of action in advance. The positional style merely prepares the transformation to a combination when the latter becomes feasible."

The Diplomacy

Diplomacy is the art and practice of conducting negotiations between representatives of groups or states. It usually refers to international diplomacy, the conduct of international relations through the intercession of professional diplomats with regard to issues of peace-making, trade, war, economics and culture. International treaties are usually negotiated by diplomats prior to endorsement by national politicians.

The word stems from the Greek word *"diploma"*, which literally means 'folded in two'. In ancient Greece, a diploma was a certificate certifying completion of a course of study, typically folded in two. In the days of the Roman Empire, the word *"diploma"* was used to describe official travel documents, such as passports and passes for imperial roads, that were stamped on double metal plates. Later, the meaning was extended to cover other official documents such as treaties with foreign tribes. In the 1700s the French called their body of officials attached to foreign legations the corps *"diplomatique"*. The word *"diplomacy"* was first introduced into the English language by Edmund Burke in 1796, based on the French word *"diplomatie"*.

In an informal or social sense, diplomacy is the employment of tact to gain strategic advantage or to find mutually acceptable solutions to a common challenge, one set of tools being the phrasing of statements in a non-confrontational, or polite manner.

Diplomats and Diplomatic Missions

A diplomat is someone involved in diplomacy; the collective term for a group of diplomats from a single country who reside in another country is a diplomatic mission. Ambassador is the most senior diplomatic rank; a diplomatic mission headed by an ambassador is known as an embassy, with the exception of permanent missions at the United Nations, the Organisation of

American States, or other multilateral organisations, which are also headed by ambassadors. The collective body of all diplomats of particular country is called that country's diplomatic service. The collective body of all diplomats assigned to a particular country is the diplomatic corps.

The Background

Europe

The ability to practice diplomacy is one of the defining elements of a state, and diplomacy has been practiced since the first city-states were formed millennia ago. For most of human history diplomats were sent only for specific negotiations, and would return immediately after their mission concluded. Diplomats were usually relatives of the ruling family or of very high rank in order to give them legitimacy when they sought to negotiate with the other state.

One notable exception involved the relationship between the Pope and the Byzantine Emperor; papal agents, called *apocrisiarii*, were permanently resident in Constantinople. After the 8th century, however, conflicts between the Pope and Emperor (such as the Iconoclastic controversy) led to the breaking of close ties.

Modern diplomacy's origins are often traced to the states of Northern Italy in the early Renaissance, with the first embassies being established in the 13th century. Milan played a leading role, especially under Francesco Sforza who established permanent embassies to the other city states of Northern Italy. It was in Italy that many of the traditions of modern diplomacy began, such as the presentation of an ambassador's credentials to the head of state.

From Italy the practice was spread to the other European powers. Milan was the first to send a representative to the court of France in 1455. However, Milan refused to host French representatives fearing espionage and that the French representatives would intervene in its internal affairs. As foreign powers such as France and Spain became increasingly involved in Italian politics the need to accept emissaries was recognised. Soon the major European powers were exchanging representatives. Spain was the first to send a permanent representative; it appointed an ambassador to the Court of England in 1487. By the late 16th century, permanent missions became customary. The Holy Roman Emperor, however, did not regularly send permanent legates, as they could not represent the interests of all the German princes (who were in theory subordinate to the Emperor, but in practice independent).

During that period the rules of modern diplomacy were further developed. The top rank of representatives was an ambassador. At that time an ambassador was a nobleman, the rank of the noble assigned varying with the prestige of the country he was delegated to. Strict standards developed for ambassadors, requiring they have large residences, host lavish parties, and play an important role in the court life of their host nation.

In Rome, the most prized posting for a Catholic ambassador, the French and Spanish representatives would have a retinue of up to a hundred. Even in smaller posts, ambassadors were very expensive. Smaller states would send and receive envoys, who were a rung below ambassador. Somewhere between the two was the position of minister plenipotentiary.

Diplomacy was a complex affair, even more so than now. The ambassadors from each state were ranked by complex levels of precedence that were much disputed. States were normally ranked by the title of the sovereign; for Catholic nations the emissary from the Vatican was paramount, then those from the kingdoms, then those from duchies and principalities. Representatives from republics were ranked the lowest. Determining precedence between two kingdoms depended on a number of factors that often fluctuated, leading to near-constant squabbling.

Ambassadors, nobles with little foreign experience and no expectation of a career in diplomacy, needed to be supported by large embassy staff. These professionals would be sent on longer assignments and would be far more knowledgeable than the higher-ranking officials about the host country. Embassy staff would include a wide range of employees, including some dedicated to espionage. The need for skilled individuals to staff embassies was met by the graduates of universities, and this led to a great increase in the study of international law, modern languages, and history at universities throughout Europe.

At the same time, permanent foreign ministries began to be established in almost all European states to coordinate embassies and their staffs. These ministries were still far from their modern form, and many of them had extraneous internal responsibilities. Britain had two departments with frequently overlapping powers until 1782. They were also far smaller than they are currently. France, which boasted the largest foreign affairs department, had only some 70 full-time employees in the 1780s.

The elements of modern diplomacy slowly spread to Eastern Europe and Russia, arriving by the early 18th century. The entire edifice would be greatly disrupted by the French Revolution and the subsequent years of warfare. The revolution would see commoners take over the diplomacy of the French state, and of those conquered by revolutionary armies. Ranks of precedence were abolished. Napoleon also refused to acknowledge diplomatic immunity, imprisoning several British diplomats accused of scheming against France.

After the fall of Napoleon, the Congress of Vienna of 1815 established an international system of diplomatic rank. Disputes on precedence among nations (and therefore the appropriate diplomatic ranks used) persisted for over a century until after World War II, when the rank of ambassador became the norm. In between that time, figures such as the German Chancellor Otto von Bismark were renowned for international diplomacy.

Asia

Diplomatic relations within the Early Modern era of Asia were depicted as an environment of prestige and Status. It was maintained that one must be of noble ancestry in order to represent an autonomous state within the international arena. Therefore, the position of diplomat was often revered as an element of the elitist class within Asia. A state's ability to practice diplomacy has been one of the underlying defining characteristics of an autonomous state. It is this practice that has been employed since the conception of the first city-states within the international spectrum. Diplomats in Asia were originally sent only for the purpose of negotiation. They would be required to immediately return after their task was completed. The majority of diplomats initially constituted the relatives of the ruling family. A high rank was bestowed upon them in order to present a sense of legitimacy with regards to their presence. Italy, the Ottoman Empire, and China were the first real states that perpetuated environments of diplomacy. During the early modern era diplomacy evolved to become a crucial element of international relations within the Mediterranean and Asia.

Ancient India, with its kingdoms and dynasties, had a long tradition of diplomacy. The oldest treatise on statecraft and diplomacy, *Arthashastra*, is attributed to Kautilya (also known as Chanakya), who was the principal adviser to Chandra Gupta Maurya, the founder of the Maurya dynasty who ruled in the 3rd century BC, (whose capital was Patliputra, today's Patna, the chief city of Bihar state). *Arthashastra* is a complete work on the art of kingship, with long chapters on taxation and on the raising and maintenance of armies.

It also incorporates a theory of diplomacy, of how in a situation of mutually contesting kingdoms, the wise king build alliances and tries to checkmate his adversaries. The envoys sent at the time to the courts of other kingdoms tended to reside for extended periods of time, and *Arthashastra* contains advice on the deportment of the envoy, including the trenchant suggestion that 'he should sleep alone'. The highest morality for the king is that his kingdom should prosper.

5

Bargaining and Agreements

Bargaining or haggling is a type of negotiation in which the buyer and seller of a good or service dispute the price which will be paid and the exact nature of the transaction that will take place, and eventually come to an agreement. Bargaining is an alternative pricing strategy to fixed prices. Optimally, if it costs the retailer nothing to engage and allow bargaining, he can divine the buyer's willingness to spend. It allows for capturing more consumer surplus as it allows price discrimination, a process whereby a seller can charge a higher price to one buyer who is more eager (by being richer or more desperate). Haggling has largely disappeared in parts of the world where the cost to haggle exceeds the gain to retailers for most common retail items. However, for expensive goods sold to uninformed buyers such as automobiles, bargaining can remain commonplace.

Bargaining is also the third stage of the Kubler-Ross model (commonly known as the Stages of Dying).

Dickering refers to the same process, albeit with a slight negative (petty) connotation.

Contexts, where Bargaining is Allowed

Not all transactions are open to bargaining. Both religious beliefs and regional custom may determine whether or not the seller is willing to bargain.

Regional Differences

In North America and Europe bargaining is restricted to expensive or one-of-a-kind items (automobiles, jewellery, art, real estate, trade sales of businesses) and informal sales settings such as flea markets and garage sales. In other regions of the world bargaining may be the norm even for small commercial transactions. In almost all large complex business negotiations, a certain amount of bargaining takes place. One simplified 'western' way to decide when it's time to bargain is to break negotiation into two stages: creating value and claiming value. Claiming value is another phrase for bargaining. Many cultures take offence when they perceive the other side as having started bargaining too soon. This offence is usually as a result of their wanting to first create value for longer before they bargain together.

The Chinese culture by contrast places a much higher value on taking time to build a business relationship before starting to create value or bargain. Not understanding when to start bargaining has ruined many a otherwise positive business negotiation.

In areas where bargaining at the retail level is common, the option to bargain often depends on the presence of the store's owner. A chain store managed by clerks is more likely to use fixed pricing than an independent store managed by an owner or one of owner's trusted employees.

The store's ambiance may also be used to signal whether or not bargaining is appropriate. For instance, a comfortable and air-conditioned store with posted prices usually do not allow bargaining, but a stall in a bazaar or marketplace may. Supermarkets and other chain stores almost never allow bargaining. However, the importance of ambiance may depend on the cultural commitment to bargaining. In Israel, prices on day-to-day items (clothing, toiletries) may be negotiable even in a Western style store manned by a clerk.

In India, a sign posted with the phrase fixed price indicates that bargaining is not allowed, although quite often this is not the case.

Religious Differences

Quakers require fixed price contracts.

Traditionally, Jews had a limit on the allowable profit margin. Limits were also placed on renegotiations of a price for services.

Various Theories

Behavioural Theory

The personality theory in bargaining emphasises that the type of personalities determine the bargaining process and its outcome. A popular behavioural theory deals with a distinction between hard-liners and soft-liners. Various research papers refer to hard-liners as warriors, while soft-liners are shopkeepers.

Game Theory

Bargaining games refer to situations where two or more players must reach agreement regarding how to distribute an object or monetary amount. Each player prefers to reach an agreement in these games, rather than abstain from doing so; however, each prefers that agreement which most favours his interests. Examples of such situations would be the bargaining involved in a labour union and the directors of a company negotiating wage increases, the dispute between two communities about the distribution of a common territory or the conditions under which two countries can start a programme of nuclear disarmament. Analysing these kinds of problem looks for a solution specifying which component in dispute will correspond to each party involved.

Players in a bargaining problem can bargain for the objective as a whole at a precise moment in time. The problem can also be divided so that parts of the whole objective become subject to bargaining during different stages.

In a classical bargaining problem the result is an agreement reached between all interested parties, or the status quo of the problem. It is clear that studying how individual parties make their decisions is insufficient for predicting what agreement will be reached. However, classical bargaining theory assumes that each participant in a bargaining process will choose between possible agreements, following the conduct predicted by the rational choice model. It is particularly assumed that each player's preferences regarding the possible agreements can be represented by a von Neumann-Morgenstern utility function.

Nash (1950) defines a classical bargaining problem as being a set of joint allocations of utility, some of which will correspond to that the players would obtain if they reach an agreement, and another which represents what they would get if they failed to do so.

A bargaining game for two players is defined as a pair (F, d) where F is the set of possible joint utility allocations (possible agreements), and d is the disagreement point.

For the definition of a specific bargaining solution is usual to follow Nash's proposal, setting out the axioms this solution should satisfy. Some of the most frequent axioms used in the building of bargaining solutions are efficiency, symmetry, independence of irrelevant alternatives, scalar invariance, monotonicity, etc.

The Nash Bargaining Solution is the bargaining solution which maximises the product of agent's utilities on the bargaining set.

The Nash Bargaining Solution, however, only deals with the simplest structure of bargaining. It is not dynamic (failing to deal with how Pareto outcomes are achieved). Instead for situations where the structure of the bargaining game is important, a more mainstream game theoretic approach is useful. This can allow player's preferences over time and risk to be incorporated into the solution of bargaining games. It can also show how the detail can matter. For example the Nash Bargaining Solution for Prisoners' Dilemma is different from the Nash equilibrium.

Processual Theory

This theory isolates distinctive elements of the bargaining chronology in order to better understand the complexity of the negotiating process. Several key features of the processual theory include:

- Bargaining range
- Critical risk
- Security point
- Toughness dilemma

Integrative Theory

Integrative bargaining (also called "interest-based bargaining," "win-win bargaining") is a negotiation strategy in which parties collaborate to find a "win-win" solution to their dispute. This strategy focuses on developing mutually beneficial agreements based on the interests of the disputants. Interests include the needs, desires, concerns, and fears important to each side. They are the underlying reasons why people become involved in a conflict.

"Integrative refers to the potential for the parties' interests to be (combined) in ways that create joint value or enlarge the pie." Potential for integration only exists when there are multiple issues involved in the negotiation. This is because the parties must be able to make trade-offs across issues in order for both sides to be satisfied with the outcome.

Narrative Theory

A very different approach to conceptualising bargaining is as co-construction of a social narrative, where narrative, rather than economic logic drives the outcome.

Automated Bargaining

When a bargaining situation is complex, finding Nash equilibrium will be difficult using game theory. Evolutionary computation methods have been designed for automated bargaining, and demonstrated efficient and effective for approximating Nash equilibrium.

Best Alternative to a Negotiated Agreement

In negotiation theory, the best alternative to a negotiated agreement or BATNA is the course of action that will be taken by a party if the current negotiations fail and an agreement cannot be reached. BATNA is the key focus and the driving force behind a successful negotiator. Not to confuse BATNA with the reservation point which can also be referred to as the walkaway point. A party should generally not accept a worse resolution than its BATNA. Care should be taken, however, to ensure that deals are accurately valued, taking into account all considerations, such as relationship value, time value of money and the likelihood that the other party will live up to their side of the bargain. These other considerations are often difficult to value, since they are frequently based on uncertain or qualitative considerations, rather than easily measurable and quantifiable factors.

The BATNA is often seen by negotiators not as a safety net, but rather as a point of leverage in negotiations. Although a negotiator's alternative options should, in theory, be straightforward to evaluate, the effort to understand which alternative represents a party's BATNA is often not invested. Options need to be real and actionable to be of value, however, without the investment of time, options will frequently be included that fail on one of these criteria. A Programme on Negotiation Executive Seminar experiment and other experiments have demonstrated that most managers overestimate their BATNA whilst simultaneously investing too little time into researching their real options. This can result in poor or faulty decision-making and negotiating outcomes.

BATNA was developed by negotiation researchers Roger Fisher and William Ury of the Harvard Programme on Negotiation (PON), in their series of books on Principled Negotiation that started with *Getting to YES*. Nobel Laureate John Forbes Nash has included such ideas in his early undergraduate research.

The following example illustrate the basic principles of identifying the BATNA and how to use it in further negotiations to help value other offers.

Examples

Selling a Car: If I have a written offer from a dealer to buy my car for $100, then my BATNA when dealing with other potential purchasers would be $100, since I can get $100 for my car even without reaching an agreement with such alternative purchaser.

In this example, other offers that illustrate the difficulty of valuing qualitative factors might include:

- An offer of $90 by a close relative (is the goodwill generated worth $10 or more?);
- An offer of $125 in 45 days (what are the chances of this future commitment falling through, and would my prior BATNA ($100) still be available if it did?);
- An offer from another dealer to offset $150 against the price of a new car (do I want to buy a new car right now, the offered car in particular? Also, is the probably minuscule reduction in monthly payments worth $100 to me today?).

Purchasing: Consider the following business example: Company one can choose to buy from companies two, three and four — but companies two, three and four can only sell to company one. Company one can use their powerful BATNA position to leverage a better deal by playing companies two, three and four against each other. This is a common practice among purchasing and procurement managers in the business world.

Collective Bargaining

Collective Bargaining is the process whereby workers organise together to meet, converse, and compromise upon the work environment with their employers. It is the practice in which union and company representatives meet to negotiate a new labour contract. In various national labour and employment law contexts, collective bargaining takes on a more specific legal meaning. In a broad sense, however, it is the coming together of workers to negotiate their employment.

A collective agreement is a labour contract between an employer and one or more unions. Collective Bargaining consists of the process of negotiation between representatives of a union and employers (represented by management, in some countries by employers' organisation) in respect of the terms and conditions of employment of employees, such as wages, hours of work, working conditions and grievance-procedures, and about the rights and responsibilities of trade unions. The parties often refer to the result of the negotiation as a *Collective Bargaining Agreement* (CBA) or as a *Collective Employment Agreement* (CEA).

Theories

A number of theories – from the fields of industrial relations, economics, political science, history and sociology (as well as the writings of activists, workers and labour organisations) – have attempted to define and explain collective bargaining. One theory suggests that collective bargaining is a human right and thus deserving of legal protection. Article 23 of the Universal Declaration of Human Rights identifies the ability to organise trade unions as a fundamental human right. Item 2(a) of the International Labour Organisation's *Declaration on Fundamental Principles and Rights at Work* defines the "freedom of association and the effective recognition of the right to collective bargaining" as an essential right of workers.

In June 2007 the Supreme Court of Canada extensively reviewed the rationale for considering collective bargaining to be a human right. In the case of *Facilities Subsector Bargaining Assn. vs British Columbia*, the Court made the following observations:

- The right to bargain collectively with an employer enhances the human dignity, liberty and autonomy of workers by giving them the opportunity to influence the establishment of workplace rules and thereby gain some control over a major aspect of their lives, namely their work.

- Collective Bargaining is not simply an instrument for pursuing external ends... rather (it) is intrinsically valuable as an experience in self-government.
- Collective Bargaining permits workers to achieve a form of workplace democracy and to ensure the rule of law in the workplace. Workers gain a voice to influence the establishment of rules that control a major aspect of their lives.

Economic theories also provide a number of models intended to explain some aspects of collective bargaining. The first is the so-called Monopoly Union Model (Dunlop, 1944), according to which the monopoly union has the power to maximise the wage rate; the firm then chooses the level of employment. This model is being abandoned by the recent literature. The second is the Right-to-Manage model, developed by the British school during the 1980s (Nickell).

In this model, the labour union and the firm bargain over the wage rate according to a typical Nash Bargaining Maximin (written as '$\Omega = U^{\beta}\Pi^{1-\beta}$, where U is the utility function of the labour union, Π the profit of the firm and β represents the bargaining power of the labour unions). The third model is called *efficient bargaining* (McDonald and Solow, 1981), where the union and the firm bargain over both wages and employment (or, more realistically, hours of work).

United Kingdom

The British academic Beatrice Webb reputedly coined the term "Collective Bargaining" in the late 19th century: the OED quotes her use of it in 1891 in *Cooperative Movement*. Webb aimed to characterise a process alternative to that of individual bargaining between an employer and individual employees. Other writers have emphasised the conflict-resolution aspects of collective bargaining, but in Britain the most important refinement in usage came from Allan Flanders, who defined Collective Bargaining as a process of rule-making leading to joint regulation in industry. Most commentators see the process of Collective Bargaining as necessarily containing an element of negotiation and hence as distinct from processes of consultation, which lack the element of negotiation and where employers determine outcomes unilaterally.

In the United Kingdom collective bargaining has become, and has received endorsement for many years as, the dominant and most appropriate means of regulating workers' terms and conditions of employment, in line with ILO Convention No. 84. However, the importance of Collective Bargaining in the United Kingdom and elsewhere in the industrialised world has declined considerably since the early 1980s. Its decline in the public sector stems in part from the growth of Review-Body arrangements provided through the Office of Manpower Economics for groups of workers, including for the majority of National Health Service staff.

Despite its significance, in the United Kingdom there remains no statutory basis for collective bargaining in the fields of learning and training, a situation that has attracted the attention of both the Trades Union Congress and members of the Royal College of Nursing. A coalition has formed which actively seeks to remedy this situation by expanding the scope of Collective Bargaining to encompass learning and training.

United States

In the United States, the National Labour Relations Act (1935) covers most collective agreements in the private sector. This act makes it illegal for employers to discriminate, spy on, harass, or terminate the employment of workers because of their union membership or retaliate against them for engaging in organising campaigns or other "concerted activities" to form "company unions", or to refuse to engage in Collective Bargaining with the union that represents their employees.

At a workplace where workers have voted for union representation, a committee of employees and union representatives negotiate a contract with the management regarding wages, hours, benefits, and other terms and conditions of employment, such as protection from termination of employment without just cause. Once the contract is agreed to by the workers' committee and management, it is then put to a vote of all workers at the workplace. If approved, the contract is usually in force for a fixed term of years, and when that term is up, it is then renegotiated between employees and management. Sometimes there are disputes over the union contract; this particularly occurs in cases of workers fired without just cause in a union workplace. These then go to arbitration, which is similar to an informal court hearing; a neutral arbitrator then rules whether the termination or other contract breach is extant, and if it is, orders that it be corrected.

In the majority of US states, workers who have elected a union may be required to contribute towards the cost of representation (such as at disciplinary hearings) if their fellow employees have negotiated a union security clause in their contract with management. Dues usually vary, but are generally 1-2 per cent of pay; however, this is usually offset by the fact that workers who are represented by unions make, on average, 30 per cent more than their non-union counterparts. Some states, especially in the south-central and south-eastern region of the US, have outlawed union security clauses; this is very controversial, as it allows individuals who benefit from the protection of union contracts to avoid paying their portion of the costs of contract negotiation. Though this sort of ban on union security clauses is often advocated by certain business interests attempting to weaken the power of unions, it can easily backfire, as the mandatory open shop, as such arrangements are called, may result in higher rates of unionisation as workers no longer may be required to pay dues to be unionised, removing one obstacle to union success in elections, and also the factor that unions in states with the open shop are required to build strong rank and file democracy among their memberships in order to sustain a high number of dues-paying members, rather than relying on the contract to bring dues in, ensuring a more active and responsive union, rather than a complacent one.

The industrial revolution brought a swell of labour organising in the US. The American Federation of Labour was formed in 1886, providing unprecedented bargaining powers for a variety of workers. The Railway Labour Act (1926) required employers to bargain collectively with unions.

In 1930, the Supreme Court, in the case of *Texas & N.O.R. Co. vs Brotherhood of Railway Clerks*, upheld the act's prohibition of employer interference in the selection of bargaining representatives. In 1962, President Kennedy signed an executive order giving public employee unions the right to collectively bargain with government agencies.

Several notable Collective Bargaining Agreements (CBAs) in the United States have involved major professional sports leagues, due in part to a history of poor relations and the vast sums of money involved. One half of the 1998-99 NBA season was cancelled due to a lockout, as was half of the 1994-95 NHL season. A breakdown in talks caused a cancellation of the entire 2004-05 NHL season, making it the first major North American sports league to lose an entire season to labour issues. Major League Baseball experienced player strikes in 1972, 1981, and 1994, the last one causing the cancellation of the World Series. In 2006 the National Football League (NFL) faced the prospect of an eventual strike, but an agreement was reached in March. The NFL did experience season-shortening strikes in 1982 and 1987, the latter of which involved the inclusion of replacement players for three games.

Continental Europe

Many continental European countries, like Austria, the Netherlands, Belgium and Sweden, have a social market economy where collective bargaining over wages, is done on the national level between national federations of labour unions and employers' organisations. In Finland, a Comprehensive Income Policy Agreement can be reached in some years. It is collective bargaining taken to its logical maximum, setting a single percentage raise for virtually all wage-earners.

For the trade unions, several sectoral federations are in charge of the collective bargaining for their affiliates.

In some countries, such as Finland, collective agreements with enough support are universally applicable, in a particular field, regardless of union membership. Effectively, the universal collective agreement sets the minimum wages and other benefits, under which no employer may go with any employee, union member or not. Personal benefits can be given regardless. Contrast this with the US labour regulations where in non-right-to-work states all employees may be required by contract to join the majority union after employment, and then must be paid a uniform contract wage without variation.

In France, collective bargaining became legal with the Matignon agreements passed in 1936 by the Popular Front government.

Bargaining Unit

A bargaining unit in labour relations is a group of employees with a clear and identifiable community of interests who are (under US law) represented by a single labour union in collective bargaining and other dealings with management. Examples would be "non-management professors"; "law enforcement professionals"; "blue-collar workers"; "clerical and administrative employees"; etc. Geographic location as well as the number of facilities included in bargaining units can be at issue during representation cases.

The size of a company does not relate to the size of a bargaining unit. Bargaining units must consist of at least 3 employees, and must have the support of a majority of employees in the bargaining unit. However, the bargaining unit could be a small portion of a large company, where no other employees are members of a union.

Collective Bargaining Convention

Collective Bargaining Convention, 1981 is an International Labour Organisation Convention.

It was established in 1981, with the preamble stating:

Having decided upon the adoption of certain proposals with regard to the promotion of collective bargaining..

Enterprise Bargaining Agreement

An Enterprise Bargaining Agreement (EBA) consists of a collective industrial agreement between either:

1. an employer and a trade union acting on behalf of employees, or;
2. an employer and employees acting for themselves.

On the one hand collective agreements, at least in principle, benefit employers, as they allow for improved "flexibility" in such areas as ordinary hours, flat rates of hourly pay, and performance-related conditions.

On the other hand collective agreements benefit workers, as they usually provide higher pay, bonuses, additional leave and enhanced entitlements (such as redundancy pay) than an award does.

EBAs in Australia

Unlike awards, which provide similar standards for all workers in the entire industry covered by a specific award, collective agreements usually apply only to workers for one employer — although on occasion a short-term collaborative agreement (for example, on a building-site) yields a multi-employer/employee agreement.

Parties endorse proposed Enterprise Bargaining Agreements between themselves (in the case of employers the matter goes to a vote). The Australian Industrial Relations Commission then certifies them. (With the introduction of Work Choices, agreements now renamed "collective workplace agreements" are lodged with the Workplace Authority and are checked for breaches of the Act.)

History of Enterprise Bargaining Agreements

The Federal Keating government of 1991-1996 introduced enterprise bargaining agreements into the Australian industrial scene.

Use of Enterprise Bargaining Agreements

Enterprise agreements have proved quite popular; on 30th of June 2006, 14383 Collective Agreements were active. June Trends in Enterprise Bargaining.

In practice they served to complement awards, and in combination they became the basic mechanisms for setting wages and conditions in Australia. A standard Enterprise Bargaining Agreement would last for three years.

EBAs had one unique feature in Australia: whilst negotiating a federal enterprise bargaining agreement, a group of employees or a trade union could, without legal penalties, undertake industrial action (including strikes) in pursuit of their claims.

Issues regarding Enterprise Bargaining Agreements

A major legal question associated with Enterprise Agreements stemmed from the High Court of Australia's decision in the case of Electrolux v The Australian Workers' Union. The question revolved around what these industrial instruments could cover. The Australian Industrial Relations Commission determined the matter in 2005 in the Three certified agreements case.

Future of EBAs in Australian Industrial Law

In the context of Australian labour law, the industrial reform of 2005 - 2006, known as "Work Choices" (with its corresponding amendments to the Workplace Relations Act (1996)) changed the name of such agreement documents to "Collective Agreement". State industrial legislation can also prescribe collective agreements, but the enactment of the Work Choices reform will make such agreements less likely to occur.

Parties to Australian federal collective agreements now lodge and certify these with the Workplace Authority. At state level, the appropriate state Industrial Relations Commission certifies state agreements.

Mutual Gains Bargaining

Mutual Gains Bargaining (MGB) is an approach to collective bargaining intended to reach *win-win* outcomes for the negotiating parties.

Instead of the traditional adversarial (*win-lose*) approach (aka positional bargaining), the mutual gains approach is quite similar to *Principled Negotiation* (first described by Roger Fisher in his book *Getting to YES*), where the goal is to reach a sustainable (i.e., lasting) agreement that both parties (or all parties in a multiparty negotiation) can live with and support.

Mutual Gains Bargaining has been used successfully in such areas as labour-management relations and environmental negotiations.

Some Principles of MGB

- Both sides have legitimate interests to be recognised and advanced.
- Approach the issues as problems to be solved.
- Listening builds trust.
- Enlarge the pie.
- Seek sustainable alternatives.

6

The Arbitration

Nations sometimes resort to international arbitration when faced with a specific question or point of contention in need of resolution. For most of history, there were no official or formal procedures for such proceedings. They were generally accepted to abide by general principles and protocols related to international law and justice.

Sometimes these took the form of formal arbitrations and mediations. In such cases a commission of diplomats might be convened to hear all sides of an issue, and to come some sort of ruling based on international law.

In the modern era, much of this work is often carried out by the International Court of Justice at the Hague, or other formal commissions, agencies and tribunals, working under the United Nations. Below are some examples.

- Hay-Herbert Treaty Enacted after the United States and Britain submitted a dispute to international mediation about the US-Canadian border.

Role of Conferences

Other times, resolutions were sought through the convening of international conferences. In such cases, there are fewer ground rules, and fewer formal applications of international law. However, participants are expected to guide themselves through principles of international fairness, logic, and protocol.

Some examples of these formal conferences are:

- *Congress of Vienna (1815):* After Napoleon was defeated, there were many diplomatic questions waiting to be resolved. This included the shape of the map of Europe, the disposition of political and nationalist claims of various ethnic groups and nationalities wishing to have some political autonomy, and the resolution of various claims by various European powers.
- The Congress of Berlin (June 13 - July 13, 1878) was a meeting of the European Great Powers' and the Ottoman Empire's leading statesmen in Berlin in 1878. In the wake of the Russo-Turkish War, 1877-78, the meeting's aim was to reorganise conditions in the Balkans.

Significance of Negotiations

Sometimes nations convene official negotiation processes to settle an issue or dispute between several nations which are parties to a dispute. These are similar to the conferences mentioned above, as there are technically no established rules or procedures. However, there are general principles and precedents which help define a course for such proceedings.

Some examples are:

- Camp David accord Convened in 1978 by President Jimmy Carter of the United States, at Camp David to reach an agreement between Prime Minister Mechaem Begin of Israel and President Anwar Sadat of Egypt. After weeks of negotiation, agreement was reached and the accords were signed, later leading directly to the Israel-Egypt Peace Treaty of 1979.
- Treaty of Portsmouth Enacted after President Theodore Roosevelt brought together the delegates from Russia and Japan, to settle the Russo-Japanese War. Roosevelt's personal intervention settled the conflict, and caused him to win the Nobel peace prize.

Diplomatic Recognition

Diplomatic Recognition is an important factor in determining whether a nation is an independent state. Receiving recognition is often difficult, even for countries which are fully sovereign. For many decades after becoming independent, even many of the closest allies of the Dutch Republic refused to grant it full recognition. Today there are a number of independent entities without widespread diplomatic recognition, most notably the Republic of China on Taiwan.

Since the 1970s, most nations have stopped officially recognising the ROC's existence on Taiwan, at the insistence of the People's Republic of China. Currently, the United States and other nations maintain informal relations through *de facto* embassies, with names such as the American Institute in Taiwan. Similarly, Taiwan's *de facto* embassies abroad are known by names such as the Taipei Economic and Cultural Representative Office. This was not always the case, with the US maintaining official diplomatic ties with the ROC, recognising it as the sole and legitimate government of all of China until 1979, when these relations were broken off as a condition for establishing official relations with Communist China.

The Palestinian National Authority has its own diplomatic service, however, Palestinian representatives in most Western countries are not accorded diplomatic immunity, and their missions are referred to as Delegations General.

Other unrecognised regions which claim independence include Abkhazia, Transnistria, Somaliland, South Ossetia, Nagorno Karabakh, and the Turkish Republic of Northern Cyprus. Lacking the economic and political importance of Taiwan, these nations tend to be much more diplomatically isolated.

Though used as a factor in judging sovereignty, Article 3 of the Montevideo Convention states, "The political existence of the state is independent of recognition by other states."

Informal Diplomacy

Informal diplomacy (sometimes called *Track II diplomacy*) has been used for centuries to communicate between powers. Most diplomats work to recruit figures in other nations who might be able to give informal access to a country's leadership.

In some situations, such as between the United States and the People's Republic of China a large amount of diplomacy is done through semi-formal channels using interlocutors such as academic members of thinktanks. This occurs in situations where governments wish to express intentions or to suggest methods of resolving a diplomatic situation, but do not wish to express a formal position.

Track II diplomacy is a specific kind of informal diplomacy, in which non-officials (academic scholars, retired civil and military officials, public figures, social activists) engage in dialogue, with the aim of conflict resolution, or confidence-building. Sometimes governments may fund such Track II exchanges. Sometimes the exchanges may have no connection at all with governments, or may even act in defiance of governments; such exchanges are called *Track III*.

Paradiplomacy

Paradiplomacy refers to the international relations conducted by subnational, regional, local or non-central governments. The most ordinary case of paradiplomatic relation refer to cooperation between bordering political entities. However, interest of federal states, provinces, regions, etc., may extend over to different regions or to issues gathering local governments in multilateral fora worldwide. Some non-central governments may be allowed to negotiate and enter into agreement with foreign central states.

Cultural Diplomacy

Cultural Diplomacy is a part of diplomacy. It alludes to a new way of making diplomacy by involving new non-governmental and non-professional actors in the making of diplomacy. In the frame of globalisation, culture plays a major role in the definition of identity and in the relations between people. Joseph Nye points out the importance of having a *soft power* besides a *hard power*. When Classical Diplomacy fails, a better knowledge can help bridging the gap between different cultures. Cultural Diplomacy becomes a subject of academic studies based on historical essays on the United States, Europe, and the Cold War.

Dispute Resolution

Dispute resolution is the process of resolving disputes between parties.

Methods

Methods of Dispute Resolution include:

- lawsuits (litigation);
- arbitration;
- collaborative law;
- mediation;
- conciliation;
- many types of negotiation; and
- facilitation.

One could theoretically include violence or even war as part of this spectrum, but dispute resolution practitioners do not usually do so; violence rarely ends disputes effectively, and indeed, often only escalates them. Some individuals, notably Joseph Stalin, have stated that all problems emanate from man, and absent man, no problems ensue. Hence, violence could theoretically end disputes, but alongside it, life.

Dispute resolution processes fall into two major types:

1. Adjudicative processes, such as litigation or arbitration, in which a judge, jury or arbitrator determines the outcome.
2. Consensual processes, such as collaborative law, mediation, conciliation, or negotiation, in which the parties attempt to reach agreement.

Not all disputes, even those in which skilled intervention occurs, end in resolution. Such intractable disputes form a special area in dispute resolution studies.

Judicial Dispute Resolution

The legal system provides a necessary structure for the resolution of many disputes. However, some disputants will not reach agreement through a collaborative processes. Some disputes need the coercive power of the state to enforce a resolution. Perhaps more importantly, many people want a professional advocate when they become involved in a dispute, particularly if the dispute involves perceived legal rights, legal wrongdoing, or threat of legal action against them.

The most common form of Judicial Dispute Resolution is litigation. Litigation is initiated when one party files suit against another. In the United States, litigation is facilitated by the government within federal, state, and municipal courts. The proceedings are very formal and are governed by rules, such as rules of evidence and procedure, which are established by the legislature. Outcomes are decided by an impartial judge and/or jury, based on the factual questions of the case and the application law. The verdict of the court is binding, not advisory; however, both parties have the right to appeal the judgement to a higher court. Judicial Dispute Resolution is typically adversarial in nature, e.g., involving antagonistic parties or opposing interests seeking an outcome most favourable to their position.

Retired judges or private lawyers often become arbitrators or mediators; however, trained and qualified non-legal dispute resolution specialists form a growing body within the field of ADR. In the United States of America, many states now have mediation or other ADR programmes annexed to the courts, to facilitate settlement of lawsuits.

Extrajudicial Dispute Resolution

Some use the term *dispute resolution* to refer only to Alternative dispute resolution (ADR), that is, extrajudicial processes such as arbitration, collaborative law, and mediation used to resolve conflict and potential conflict between and among individuals, business entities, governmental agencies, and (in the public international law context) states. ADR generally depends on agreement by the parties to use ADR processes, either before or after a dispute has arisen. ADR has experienced steadily increasing acceptance and utilisation because of a perception of greater flexibility, costs below those of traditional litigation, and speedy resolution of disputes, among other perceived advantages. However, some have criticised these methods as taking away the right to seek redress of grievances in the courts, suggesting that extrajudicial dispute resolution may not offer the fairest way for parties not in an equal bargaining relationship, for example in a dispute between a consumer and a large corporation. In addition, in some circumstances, arbitration and other ADR processes may become as expensive as litigation or more so.

Online Dispute Resolution

Dispute Resolution can also take place on-line or by using technology in certain cases. Online Dispute Resolution, a growing field of Dispute Resolution, uses new technologies to solve disputes. Online Dispute Resolution is also called "ODR". Online Dispute Resolution or ODR also involves the application of traditional dispute resolution methods to disputes which arise online.

Expert Determination

Expert Determination is a historically accepted form of Dispute Resolution invoked when there isn't a *formulated dispute* in which the parties have defined positions that need to be subjected to arbitration, but rather both parties are in agreement that there is a need for an evaluation.

The practise itself is millennia old and well established where complex legal institutions either have not developed, or are unavailable, such as tribal societies and criminal organisations.

In the context of modern jurisprudence the word "expert" appears first in *Bottomley v Ambler* 1878 38 LT 545, this was, however, used ambiguously also referring to arbitrators having the qualification of expert. The first mention that distinguishes specifically against the practise of arbitration, and introduces the formula *"as an expert and not as an arbitrator"* was in *Dean v. Prince* 1953 Ch. 590 at 591 (misquoted) and subsequently on appeal in the year 1954 1 Ch. 409 at 415. In Contract Law, the parties are free to include a forum selection clause appointing a special referee to resolve specialised but disputed factual issues between them.

7

The Mediation

Mediation, a form of Alternative Dispute Resolution (ADR) or "Appropriate Dispute Resolution", aims to assist two (or more) disputants in reaching an agreement. The parties themselves determine the conditions of any settlements reached— rather than accepting something imposed by a third party. The disputes may involve (as parties) states, organisations, communities, individuals or other representatives with a vested interest in the outcome.

Mediators use appropriate techniques and/or skills to open and/or improve dialogue between disputants, aiming to help the parties reach an agreement (with concrete effects) on the disputed matter. Normally, all parties must view the mediator as impartial.

Disputants may use mediation in a variety of disputes, such as commercial, legal, diplomatic, workplace, community and family matters.

A third-party representative may contract and mediate between (say) unions and corporations. When a workers' union goes on strike, a dispute takes place, and the corporation hires a third party to intervene in attempt to settle a contract or agreement between the union and the corporation.

History of Mediation

The activity of mediation in itself appeared in very ancient times. Historians presume early cases in Phoenician commerce (but suppose its use in Babylon, too). The practice developed in Ancient Greece (which knew the non-marital mediator as a *proxenetas*), then in Roman civilisation, Roman law (starting from Justinian's *Digest* of 530-533 CE) recognised mediation. The Romans called mediators by a variety of names, including *internuncius, medium, intercessor, philantropus, interpolator, conciliator, interlocutor, interpres,* and finally *mediator*.

The Middle Ages regarded mediation differently, sometimes forbidding the practice or restricting its use to centralised authorities.

Some cultures regarded the mediator as a sacred figure, worthy of particular respect; and the role partly overlapped with that of traditional wise men or tribal chief.

Mediation and Conciliation

"Conciliation" sometimes serves as an umbrella-term that covers all mediation and facilitative and advisory dispute-resolution processes. Neither process determines an outcome, and both share many similarities. For example, both processes involve a neutral third-party who has no enforcing powers.

One significant difference between conciliation and mediation lies in the fact that conciliators possess expert knowledge of the domain in which they conciliate. The conciliator can make suggestions for settlement terms and can give advice on the subject-matter. Conciliators may also use their role to actively encourage the parties to come to a resolution. In certain types of dispute the conciliator has a duty to provide legal information. This helps any agreement reached to comply with any relevant statutory framework pertaining to the dispute. Therefore, conciliation may include an advisory aspect.

Mediation works purely facilitatively: the practitioner has no advisory role. Instead, a mediator seeks to help parties to develop a shared understanding of the conflict and to work towards building a practical and lasting resolution.

Several different styles of mediation exist: evaluative, facilitative, and transformative. Evaluative mediation has somewhat of an advisory role in that its practitioners evaluate the strengths and weaknesses of each side's argument should they go to court; whereas facilitative mediators and transformative mediators do not do this.

Furthermore, the definitions of mediation used by the different styles of mediation differ in that evaluative mediation has the main drive and goal of settlement, while transformative mediation, in contrast, looks at conflict as a crisis in communication and seeks to help resolve the conflict, thereby allowing people to feel empowered in themselves and better about each other. The agreement that arises from this type of mediation occurs as a natural outcome of the resolution of conflict.

Both mediation and conciliation serve to identify the disputed issues and to generate options that help disputants reach a mutually-satisfactory resolution. They both offer relatively flexible processes; and any settlement reached should have the agreement of all parties. This contrasts with litigation, which normally settles the dispute in favour of the party with the strongest legal argument. In-between the two operates collaborative law, which uses a facilitative process where each party has counsel.

Why Choose Mediation?

Several reasons exist for choosing mediation over other channels of dispute resolution (such as those involving attorneys and courts).

- Parties to a dispute may choose mediation as (often) a less expensive route to follow for dispute resolution. While a mediator may charge a fee comparable to that of an attorney, the mediation process generally takes much less time than moving a case through standard legal channels. While a case in the hands of a lawyer or filed in court may take months or even years to resolve, a case in mediation usually achieves a resolution in a matter of hours. Taking less time means expending less money on hourly fees and costs.
- Mediation offers a confidential process. While court hearings of cases happen in public, whatever happens in mediation remains strictly confidential. No one but the parties to the dispute and the mediator(s) know what has gone on in the mediation forum. In fact, confidentiality in mediation has

such importance that in most cases the legal system cannot force a mediator to testify in court as to the content or progress of a mediation. Many mediators actually destroy their notes taken during a mediation once that mediation has finished. The only exceptions to such strict confidentiality usually involve child abuse or actual or threatened criminal acts.

- Mediation offers multiple and flexible possibilities for resolving a dispute and for the control the parties have over the resolution. In a case filed in court, the parties will obtain a resolution, but a resolution thrust upon the parties by the judge or jury. The result probably will leave neither party to the dispute totally happy.
- In mediation, on the other hand, the parties have control over the resolution, and the resolution can be unique to the dispute. Often, solutions developed by the parties are ones that a judge or jury could not provide. Thus, mediation is more likely to produce a result that is mutually agreeable, or win/win, for the parties. And because the result is attained by the parties working together and is mutually agreeable, the compliance with the mediated agreement is usually high. This also results in less costs, because the parties do not have to seek out the aid of an attorney to force compliance with the agreement. The mediated agreement is, however, fully enforceable in a court of law.
- The mediation process consist of a mutual endeavour. Unlike in negotiations (where parties are often entrenched in their positions), parties to a mediation usually seek out mediation because they are ready to work towards a resolution to their dispute. The mere fact that parties are willing to mediate in most circumstances means that they are ready to "move" their position. Since both parties are willing to work towards resolving the case, they are more likely to work with one another than against one another. The parties thus are amenable to understanding the other party's side and work on underlying issues to the dispute. This has the added benefit of often preserving the relationship the parties had before the dispute.

- Finally, but certainly not least, and as mentioned earlier in this section, mediation takes place with the aid of a mediator who is a neutral third party. A good mediator is trained in conflict resolution and in working with difficult situations. The good mediator is likely to work as much with the emotional aspects and relationship aspects of a case as he or she is to work on the "topical" issues of the matter. The mediator, as a neutral, gives no legal advice, but guides the parties through the problem solving process. The mediator may or may not suggest alternative solutions to the dispute. Whether he or she offers advice or not, the trained mediator helps the parties think "outside of the box" for possible solutions to the dispute, thus enabling the parties to find the avenue to dispute resolution that suits them best.

Mediation in Franchising Sector

Franchise-agreements represent ongoing commercial agreements between the contracting parties. The agreements usually have elements of an imbalance of bargaining power and of an imbalance of business experience between the franchisee and franchisor; and the parties also face many external commercial pressures.

The franchising code of conduct functions as a mandatory code under the TPA. All franchise agreements must have a clause that requires dispute resolution. Mediation in this field works because it can identify alternatives for the parties and then the parties can work together to solve the dispute. This type of mediation has formal procedures: for example: whoever wishes to initiate the mediation must advise the respondent in writing, outlining the nature of the dispute, and they will then have three weeks to agree to a method of resolving the dispute otherwise they may go to mediation.

Early Neutral Evaluation and Mediation

The technique of Early Neutral Evaluation (ENE) provides early focus in complex commercial disputes, and — based on that focus — offers a basis for sensible case-management or a suggested resolution of the entire case in its very early stages.

In Early Neutral Evaluation, an evaluator acts as a neutral person to assess the strengths and weaknesses of each of the parties and to discuss the same with parties jointly or in caucuses, so that parties gain awareness (via independent evaluation) of the merits of their case. In the case of mediation, solutions normally emerge from the parties themselves and mediators endeavour to find the most acceptable solution by bridging gaps between the parties.

Parties generally call on a senior counsel or on a panel with expertise and experience in the subject-matter under dispute in order to conduct ENE. One refers to such persons as "evaluators" or as "neutral persons".

Mediator Education and Training

Suitable education and training for mediators becomes a complex issue — largely due to the breadth of areas which may call on mediation as a means of dispute-resolution. Debate ensues on what constitutes adequate training on the principles of mediation as well as what personal attributes an individual needs in order to effectively carry out a mediator's role.

The educational requirements for accreditation as a mediator differ between accrediting groups and from country to country. In some cases legislation mandates these requirements; while in others professional bodies impose standards and applicants must comply prior to becoming accredited by them. Many US universities offer graduate studies in mediation, culminating in the Ph.D. or D.Med. degrees.

In Australia, for example, professionals wanting to practise in the area of family law must have tertiary qualifications in law or in social science, undertake 5 days training in mediation and engage in at least 10 hours of supervised mediation. Furthermore, they must also undertake 12 hours of mediation-education or training every 12 months.

Other institutions offer units in mediation across a number of disciplines such as law, social science, business and the humanities. In Australia not all fields of mediation-work require academic qualifications, as some deal more with practical skills rather than with theoretical knowledge: to this end membership-organisations provide training-courses to further the adoption and practice of mediation. Internationally a similar approach to the training of mediators is taken by the organisation CEDR, which trains 300 mediators a year in China, Hong Kong, India, Ireland, Nigeria, Pakistan, United Kingdom, Ukraine and elsewhere.

No legislated national or international standards on the level of education which should apply to all mediation practitioner's organisations exist. However, organisations such as the National Alternative Dispute Resolution Advisory Council (NADRAC) in Australia continue to advocate for a wide scope on such issues. Other systems apply in other jurisdictions such as Germany, which advocates a higher level of educational qualification for practitioners of mediation.

Mediator Codes of Conduct

The application of a code of conduct to the practice of mediation becomes problematic — due in part to the diverse number and type of practitioners in the field. A tendency exists for professional societies to develop their own codes of conduct, which apply to their own members. Examples of this in Australia include the mediation codes of conduct developed by the Law Societies of South Australia and Western Australia and those developed by organisations such as Institute of Arbitrators & Mediators Australia (IAMA) and LEADR for use by their members. Other organisations such as the American Centre for Conflict Resolution Institute have developed both classroom and distance learning courses which subscribe to its mission of promoting peace through education. The CPR/Georgetown Ethics Commission, the Mediation Forum of the Union International des Avocats, and the European Commission have also promulgated codes of conduct for mediators.

Writers in the field of mediation normally espouse a code of conduct that mirrors the underlying principles of the mediation process. In this respect some of the most common aspects of a mediator codes of conduct include:

- a commitment to inform participants as to the process of mediation;
- the need to adopt a neutral stance towards all parties to the mediation, revealing any potential conflicts of interest;

- the requirement for a mediator to conduct the mediation in an impartial manner;
- within the bounds of the legal framework under which the mediation is undertaken any information gained by the mediators should be treated as confidential;
- mediators should be mindful of the psychological and physical wellbeing of all the mediations participants;
- mediators should not offer legal advice, rather they should direct participants to appropriate sources for the provision of any advice they might need;
- mediators should seek to maintain their skills by engaging in ongoing training in the mediation process; and
- mediators should practise only in those fields in which they have expertise gained by their own experience or training.

Accreditation of ADR in Australia

Australia has no national accreditation system for ADR. However, following the National Mediation Conference in May 2006, the National Mediation Accreditation Standards system has apparently started to move to its implementation phase.

ADR practitioners recognise that mediators (as distinct from arbitrators or conciliators) need to be recognised as having professional accreditations the most. There are a range of organisations within Australia that do have extensive and comprehensive accreditations for mediators but people that use mediation are unsure as to what level of accreditation is required for the quality of service that they receive. Standards will tend to vary according to the specific mediation and the level of specificity that is desired. Due to the wide range of ADR processes that are conducted it would be very difficult to have a set of standards that could apply to all ADR processes, but standards should be developed for particular ADR processes.

Clients need the assurance that mediators have some form of ongoing assessment and training throughout their careers. Mediators must satisfy different criteria to be eligible for a variety of mediator panels. Also different mediator organisations have different ideals of what makes a good mediator which in turn reflects the training and accreditation of that particular organisation. Selection processes for ADR practitioners are based on the needs of the service, but a problem is posed when organisations, such as the court want to refer a client to mediation and they usually have to rely on their in-house mediators or rely on word of mouth. There are inconsistent standards. A national accreditation system could very well enhance the quality and ethics of mediation and lead mediation to become more accountable. There is a need for a unified accreditation system for mediators across Australia to establish clarity and consistency.

Uses of Mediation

One core problem in the dispute-resolution process involves the determination of what the parties actually dispute. Through the process of mediation participants can agree to the scope of the dispute or issues requiring resolution. Examples of this use of mediation in the Australian jurisdiction include narrowing the scope of legal pleadings and its use in industrial and environmental disputes.

Definition of the nature of a dispute can often clarify the process of determining what method will best suit its resolution.

One of the primary uses of mediation involves parties using the mediation process to define the issues, develop options and achieve a mutually-agreed resolution.

Australia has incorporated mediation extensively into the dispute-settlement process of family law and into the latest round of reforms concerning industrial relations under the Work Choices amendments to the Workplace Relations Act.

Where prospects exist of an ongoing disputation between parties brought on by irreconcilable differences (stemming from such things as a clash of religious or cultural beliefs), mediation can serve as a mechanism to foster communication and interaction.

Mediation can function not only as a tool for dispute resolution but also as a means of dispute prevention. Mediation can be used to facilitate the process of contract negotiation by the identification of mutual interests and the promotion of effective communication between the two parties. Examples of this use of mediation can be seen in recent enterprise bargaining negotiations within Australia.

Governments can also use mediation to inform and to seek input from stakeholders in formulation or fact-seeking aspects of policy-making. Mediation in wider aspect can also serve to prevent conflict or to develop mechanisms to address conflicts as they arise.

Native-title Mediation in Australia

In response to the Mabo decision by the High Court of Australia, the Australian Government sought to alleviate the concerns of a wide section of the population and industry on the decisions implications on land tenure and use by enacting the Native Title Act 1993 (Cth). A cornerstone of the act is the use of mediation as a mechanism to determine future native title rights within Australia.

Although not barring litigation, the Act seeks to promote mediation through a process incorporating the Federal Court and the National Native Title Tribunal (NNTT). This is seen as having a better long tern success by providing flexible and practical solutions to the needs of the various stakeholders.

The extensive use of mediation in the resolution of native title matters does not stop the referral of matters to the courts for resolution, nor is mediation precluded from occurring whilst legal challenges are being pursued. A recent case where Native Title rights were found exist over a large portion of the City of Perth has seen the simultaneous use of mediation and formal legal appeals processes.

A key feature of Native Title Mediation involves the use of Indigenous Land Use Agreements (ILUAs). These binding agreements are negotiated between native title claimant groups and others such as pastoralists, miners and local governments and cover aspects of the use of the land and any future act such as the granting of mining leases.

Some of the features of native title mediation which distinguish it from other forms include the likelihood of lengthy negotiation time frames, the number of parties (ranging on occasion into the hundreds) and that statutory and case law prescriptions constrain some aspects of the negotiations.

Philosophy of Mediation

The Uses of Mediation in Preventing Conflicts

Mediation is a very usual tool, adaptable to anticipate problems, grievances and difficulties between parties before the conflict may arise. This has potential applications in large and private sector organisations, particularly where they are subject to excessive change, competition and economic pressure. A key way mediation is used to prevent these conflicts is complaint handling and management. This is a conflict prevention mechanism designed to handle a complaint effectively at first contact and to minimise the possibility of it developing into a dispute. According to Charlton (2000) a person who undertakes this role is commonly known as a "dispute preventer".

While the corporate sector may provide one area in which to use the mediation process for preventing conflicts, dealing with everyday life's disputes provides another. This is no more evident in neighbourhood conflict. One's behaviour affects one's neighbours, just as what they do affects you. The key way to prevent conflicts with neighbours is to behave as a good neighbour oneself. Spencer and Altobelli (2005) believe simple consideration and conversation with neighbours helps achieve a peaceful coexistence. Making it is easier for you to live as privately or as sociably as you wish. Ideal suggestions for consideration in preventing conflicts between neighbours include:

- meeting one's neighbours;
- keeping one's neighbours informed;
- awareness of differences;
- appreciation;
- consideration of one's neighbours' points of view;
- showing candidness;
- communicating; and
- demonstrating respect.

One can also employ mediation to reduce or prevent violence in sports and in schools, using peers as mediators is a process known as "peer mediation". This process (highlighted by Charlton provides a popular way of handling conflicts and of preventing violence in primary schools, high schools and sporting activities. Schools adopting this process often recruit and train students interested in being peer mediators.

In general, effective communication provides the ideal way to prevent and resolve any conflict; talking things over — along with listening — handles problems optimally and should ultimately avoid the dispute going to the courts.

Responsibilities regarding Confidentiality in Mediation

One of the hallmarks of mediation is that the process is strictly confidential. The mediator must inform the parties that communications between them during the intake discussions and the mediation process are to be private and confidential. In general, the information discussed can never be used as evidence in the event that the matter does not settle at mediation and proceeds to a court hearing.

Spencer and Altobelli (2005) point out it is considered common for parties entering into mediation to sign a mediation agreement document with the mediator. The parties, therefore, agree that it's a condition of being present or participating in the mediation and the document if necessary may be deemed confidential by virtue of the common law.

Confidentiality lies at the heart of mediation. It is imperative for parties to trust the process. Very few mediations will ever succeed unless the parties can communicate fully and openly without fear of compromising their case before the courts. Charlton and Dewdney (2004) highlight mediation confidentiality is seen as one of the key ingredients to encourage disputing parties to negotiate with each other in order to achieve a settlement of their dispute.

Organisations have often seen confidentiality as a reason to use mediation ahead of litigation, particularly when disputes arise in sensitive areas of their operation, or to avoid their affairs becoming publicised among business competitors, acquaintances or friends. Steps put in place during mediation to help ensure this privacy include;

1. the mediation meeting is conducted behind closed doors;
2. outsiders can only observe proceedings with both parties consent;
3. no recording of the transcript is kept; and
4. there is no external publicity on what transpired at the mediation.

There is no doubt confidentiality contributes to the success and integrity of the mediation process. However, it will be difficult for a mediator to guarantee full confidentiality protection between the parties.

Legal Implications of Mediated Agreements

Parties who enter into mediation do not forfeit any legal rights or remedies. If the mediation process does not result in settlement, each side can continue to enforce their rights through appropriate court or tribunal procedures. However, if a settlement has been reached through mediation, legal rights and obligations are affected in differing degrees. In some situations, the parties may only wish to have a memorandum or a moral force agreement put in place; these are often found in community mediations. In other instances, a more comprehensive deed of agreement is drafted and this deed serves to bring a legally binding situation. Charlton and Dewdney (2004) point out that a mediated agreement may be registered with the court to make it legally binding and it is advisable to have a lawyer prepare the form or, at the very least, to obtain independent legal advice about the proposed terms of the agreement.

Mediation has opened the door for parties in conflict to resolve their differences through non-traditional judicial forums. Over the last few decades, mediation has brought to light the processes, or alternatives to litigation, that enable parties to resolve their differences without the high cost associated with litigation. An interesting remark made by Spencer and Altobelli (2005): "Court systems are eager to introduce mandatory mediation as a means to meet their needs to reduce case loads and adversarial litigation, and participants who understand the empowerment of mediation to self-determine their own agreements are equally as eager to embrace mediation as an alternative to costly and potentially harmful litigation."

Recently mediation has come under the spotlight and the watchful eye of many state legal systems for its ability to resolve party disputes, reduce court case loads, and reduce overall legal costs. Yet while parties enter into mediation intending to preserve their legal rights and remedies, mediation may result in these rights being directly or indirectly affected. Parties that have resolved their conflict through this voluntary process and settled on an agreement should seek legal advice if they are unsure of the consequences.

Transmediation involves the process of "responding to cultural texts in a range of sign systems — art, movement, sculpture, dance, music, and so on — as well as in words."

Common Aspects of Mediation

Mediation as a process involves a third party (often an impartial third party) assisting two or more persons, ("parties" or "stakeholders") to find mutually-agreeable solutions to difficult problems.

People make use of mediation at many different levels and in multiple contexts: from minor disputes to global peace-talks. This makes it difficult to provide a general description without referring to practices in specific jurisdictions — where "mediation" may in fact have a formal definition and in some venues may require specific licenses. This section attempts only a broad introduction, referring to more specific processes (such as peace process, binding arbitration, or mindful mediation) directly in the text.

While some people loosely use the term "mediation" to mean any instance in which a third party helps people find agreement, professional mediators generally believe it essential that mediators have thorough training, competency, and continuing education. The term "mediation" also sometimes occurs incorrectly referring to arbitration; a mediator does not impose a solution on the parties, whereas an arbitrator does.

While mediation implies bringing disputing parties face-to-face with each other, the strategy of "shuttle diplomacy", where the mediator serves as a liaison between disputing parties, also sometimes occurs as an alternative.

Some of the types of disputes or decision-making that often go to mediation include the following:

Family:

- Prenuptial/Premarital agreements.
- Financial or budget disagreements.
- Separation.
- Divorce.
- Financial distribution and spousal support (alimony).
- Parenting plans (child custody and visitation).
- Eldercare issues.
- Family businesses.
- Adult sibling conflicts.
- Disputes between parents and adult children.
- Estate disputes.
- Medical ethics and end-of-life issues.

Workplace:

- Wrongful termination.
- Discrimination.
- Harassment.
- Grievances.
- Labour management.

Public disputes:

- Environmental.
- Land-use.

Disputes involving the following issues:

- Landlord/tenant.
- Homeowners' associations.
- Builders/contractors/realtors/homeowners.

- Contracts of any kind.
- Medical malpractice.
- Personal injury.
- Partnerships.
- Non-profit organisations.
- Faith communities.

Other:

- Youth (school conflicts; peer mediation).
- Violence-prevention.
- Victim-Offender mediation.

Mediation commonly includes the following aspects or stages:

- a controversy, dispute or difference of positions between people, or a need for decision-making or problem-solving;
- decision-making remaining with the parties rather than imposed by a third party;
- the willingness of the parties to negotiate a "positive" solution to their problem, and to accept a discussion about respective interests and objectives; and
- the intent to achieve a "positive" result through the facilitative help of an independent, neutral third person.

In the United States, mediator codes-of-conduct emphasise "client-directed" solutions rather than those imposed by a mediator in any way. This has become a common, definitive feature of mediation in the US and in the UK.

Mediation differs from most other adversarial resolution processes by virtue of its simplicity, informality, flexibility, and economy.

The typical mediation has no formal compulsory elements, although some common elements usually occur:

- each of the parties allowed to explain and detail their story;
- the identification of issues (usually facilitated by the mediator);
- the clarification and detailed specification of respective interests and objectives;

- the conversion of respective subjective evaluations into more objective values;
- identification of options;
- discussion and analysis of the possible effects of various solutions;
- the adjustment and the refining of the proposed solutions; and
- the memorialisation of agreements into a written draft.

Due to the particular character of this activity, each mediator uses a method of his or her own (the law does not ordinarily govern a mediator's methods), that might eventually differ markedly from the above scheme. Also, many matters do not legally require a particular form for the final agreement, while others expressly require a precisely determined form.

Most countries respect a mediator's confidentiality.

Online Mediation

Online Mediation, a sub-category of online dispute resolution, involves the application of online technology to the process of mediation. Online Mediation extends the reach of mediators to disputes between persons who are too geographically distant, or otherwise unable (for example, through disability), to attend; or where the value of the dispute does not justify the cost of a face-to-face mediation. Online Mediation can also prove useful prior to face-to-face mediation — to commence the mediation process early where urgency exists, to narrow the issues, to commence brainstorming of solutions and to prepare the parties.

Mediation in Business and Commerce

The eldest branch of mediation applies to business and commerce and still this one is the widest field of application, with reference to the number of mediators in these activities and to the economical range of total exchanged values.

The mediator in business or in commerce helps the parties to achieve the final goal of respectively buying/selling (a generic contraposition that includes all the possible varieties of the exchange of goods or rights) something at satisfactory conditions (typically in the aim of producing a bilateral contract), harmonically bringing the separate elements of the treaty to a respectively balanced equilibrium. The mediator, in ordinary practice, usually takes care of finding a positive agreement between (or among) the parties looking at the main pact as well as at the accessory pacts too, thus finding a composition of all the related aspects that might combine in the best possible way, all the *desiderata* of his clients.

Academics sometimes include this activity among the auxiliary activities of commerce and business, but it has to be recalled that it differs from the generality of the others, because of its character of independence from the parties: in an ordinary activity of agency, or in the unilateral mandate this character is obviously missing, this kind of agent merely resulting as a *longa manus* of the party that gave him his (wider or narrower) power of representation. The mediator does not obey to any of the parties, and is a third party, looking at the contraposition from an external point of view.

Subfields of commercial mediation include work in well-known specialised branches: in finance, in insurance, in ship-brokering, in real estate and in some other individual markets, mediators have specialised designations and usually obey special laws. Generally, mediators cannot practice commerce in the genre of goods in which they work as specialised mediators.

Mediation and Litigation

Mediation offers a process by which two parties work towards an agreement with the aid of a neutral third party. Litigation, however, is a process in which the courts impose binding decisions on the disputing parties in a determinative process operating at the level of legal rights and obligations (Boulle 2005). These two processes sound completely different, but both are a form of dispute resolution. Litigation is conventionally used and conventionally accepted, but mediation is slowly becoming more recognised as a successful tool in dispute resolution. Slowly these processes are becoming interdependent, as the Courts in some cases are now referring parties to mediation. In saying this, there are distinct differences between the two processes. Mediation claims to resolve many of the problems associated with litigation, such as the high costs involved, the formality of the court system and the complexity of the court process. Mediation does not create binding agreements unless the parties consent to it, and the mediator has no say in the outcome. Even though our court system and mediation have increasing connections, they still reflect different value assumptions and structural approaches towards dispute resolution.

Community Mediation

Disputes involving neighbours often have no formal dispute-resolution mechanism. Community-mediation centres generally focus on this type of neighbourhood conflict, with trained volunteers from the local community usually serving as mediators. These organisations often serve populations that cannot afford to utilise the court systems or other private ADR-providers. Many community programmes also provide mediation for disputes between landlords and tenants, members of homeowners associations, and businesses and consumers. Mediation helps the parties to repair relationships, in addition to addressing a particular substantive dispute. Agreements reached in community mediation are generally private, but in some states, such as California, the parties have the option of making their agreement enforceable in court. Many community programmes offer their services for free or at most, charge a nominal fee.

The roots of community mediation can be found in community concerns to find better ways to resolve conflicts, and efforts to improve and complement the legal system. Citizens, neighbours, religious leaders and communities became empowered, realising that they could resolve many complaints and disputes on their own in their own community through mediation. Experimental community mediation programmes using volunteer mediators began in the early 1970s in several major cities. These proved to be so successful that hundreds of other programmes were founded throughout the country in the following two decades. Community mediation programmes now flourish throughout the United States.

Competence of the Mediator

Numerous schools of thought exist on identifying the "competence" of a mediator. Where parties retain mediators to provide an evaluation of the relative strengths and weaknesses of the parties' positions, subject-matter expertise of the issues in dispute becomes a primary aspect in determining competence.

Some would argue, however, that an individual who gives an opinion about the merits or value of a case does not practise "true" mediation, and that to do so fatally compromises the alleged mediator's neutrality.

Where parties expect mediators to be process experts only (i.e., employed to use their skills to work through the mediation process without offering evaluations as to the parties' claims) competence is usually demonstrated by the ability to remain neutral and to move parties through various impasse-points in a dispute. International professional organisations continue to debate what competency means.

When to Use Mediation?

Not all disputes lend themselves well to mediation. One set of criteria for suitability is provided in *Mediation - Principles Process Practice, Boulle L. 2005.*

8

Role of Consistency

In negotiation, consistency, or the consistency principle, refers to a negotiator's strong psychological need to be consistent with prior acts and statements.

Dr. Robert Cialdini and his research team have conducted extensive research into what Cialdini refers to as the 'Consistency Principle of Persuasion'. Described in his book *Influence Science and Practice*, this principle states that people live up to what they have publicly said they will do and what they have written down. So Cialdini encourages us to have others write down their commitments as a route to having others live up to their promises.

The Contract

A contract is an exchange of promises between two or more parties to do, or refrain from doing, an act which is enforceable in a court of law. It is a binding legal agreement. That is to say, a contract is an exchange of promises for the breach of which the law will provide a remedy.

Agreement is said to be reached when an offer capable of immediate acceptance is met with a "mirror image" acceptance (i.e., an unqualified acceptance). The parties must have the necessary capacity to contract and the contract must not be either trifling, indeterminate, impossible or illegal. Contract law is based on the principle expressed in the Latin phrase *pacta sunt servanda* (usually translated "pacts must be kept", but more literally "agreements are to be kept"). Breach of contract is recognised by the law and remedies can be provided. Sometimes written contracts are required, such as when buying a house. However, most contracts can be and are made orally, such as purchasing a book or a sandwich. Contract law can be classified, as is habitual in civil law systems, as part of a general law of obligations (along with tort, unjust, enrichment or restitution).

According to legal scholar Sir John William Salmond, a contract is "an agreement creating and defining the obligations between two or more parties".

As a means of economic ordering, contract relies on the notion of consensual exchange and has been extensively discussed in broader economic, sociological and anthropological terms.

This section mainly concerns contract law in common law jurisdictions (approximately coincident with the English-speaking world and anywhere the British Empire once held sway). However, contract is a form of economic ordering common throughout the world, and different rules apply in jurisdictions applying civil law (derived from Roman law principles), Islamic law, socialist legal systems, and customary or local law.

The primacy of discussion of common law principles in writing about contract may derive from the primacy of these systems in international business. Common law jurisdictions usually offer proceedings in the English language, which has become to an extent the *lingua franca* of international business, tend to have much larger law firms than in civilian jurisdictions, able to satisfy clients that their range of legal needs can be met, and unlike civilian jurisdictions, judges in common law jurisdictions are generally senior lawyers of considerable practical experience. Another possible reason is that the common law retains a high degree of freedom of contract, with parties largely free to set their own terms, whereas civilian systems typically prescribe large parts of the contents of contracts for the parties, with no opt-out provision.

It is very common for businesses not located in common law jurisdictions to opt in to the common law through "choice of law" clauses, with the most common jurisdictions of choice probably being England and Wales and New York.

Contractual Formation

In common law systems, the five key requirements for the creation of a contract are: 1) offer and acceptance (agreement), 2) consideration, 3) an intention to create legal relations, 4) legal capacity, 5) formalities.

In civil law systems, the concept of consideration is not central. In addition, for some contracts formalities must be complied with under what is sometimes called a *statute of frauds*.

One of the most famous cases on forming a contract is *Carlill v. Carbolic Smoke Ball Company* decided in nineteenth-century England. A medical firm advertised that its new wonder drug, a smoke ball, would prevent the catching of flu by those who used it in accordance with instructions, and if it did not, buyers would receive £100. When sued, Carbolic argued the ad was not to be taken as a serious, legally binding offer. It was merely an invitation to treat, and a gimmick. But the court of appeal held that it would appear to a reasonable man that Carbolic had made a serious offer, primarily because of the reference to the £1000 deposited into the bank. People had given good "consideration" for it by going to the "distinct inconvenience" of using a faulty product. "Read the advertisement how you will, and twist it about as you will," said Lindley LJ, "here is a distinct promise expressed in language which is perfectly unmistakable".

Where a product in large quantities is advertised in a newspaper or on a poster, it may be an offer, but generally speaking it will be regarded as an invitation to treat, since even when large stock is held it is still limited, whilst the response to an advertisement may be unlimited. This was the basis of the decision in *Partridge v. Crittenden* a criminal case in which the defendant was charged with "offering for sale" bramblefinch cocks and hens.

The court held that the newspaper advertisement could only be an invitation to treat, since it could not have been intended as an offer to the world, so the defendant was not guilty of "offering" them for sale. Similarly, a display of goods in a shop window is an invitation to treat, as was held in *Fisher v. Bell* another criminal case which turned on the correct analysis of offers as against invitations to treat. In this instance the defendant was charged with "offering for sale" prohibited kinds of knife, which he had displayed in his shop window with prices attached.

The court held that this was an invitation to treat, the offer would be made by a purchaser going into the shop and asking to buy a knife, with acceptance being by the shopkeeper, which he could withhold. (The law was later amended to "exposing for sale"). A display of goods on the shelves of a self-service shop is also an invitation to treat, with the offer being made by the purchaser at the checkout and being accepted by the shop assistant operating the checkout: *Pharmaceutical Society of Great Britain v. Boots Cash Chemists (Southern) Ltd.* If the person who is to buy the advertised product is of importance, for instance because of his personality, etc., when buying land, it is regarded merely as an invitation to treat. In Carbolic Smoke Ball, the major difference was that a reward was included in the advertisement, which is a general exception to the rule and is then treated as an offer.

Offer and Acceptance

The most important feature of a contract is that one party makes an offer for an arrangement that another accepts. This can be called a 'concurrence of wills' or 'ad idem' (meeting of the minds) of two or more parties. The concept is somewhat contested. The obvious objection is that a court cannot read minds and the existence or otherwise of agreement is judged objectively, with only limited room for questioning subjective intention. Richard Austen-Baker has suggested that the perpetuation of the idea of 'meeting of minds' may come from a misunderstanding of the Latin term 'consensus ad idem', which actually means 'agreement to the same thing'. There must be evidence that the parties had each from an objective perspective engaged in conduct manifesting their assent, and a contract will be formed when the parties have met such a requirement. An objective perspective means that it is only necessary that somebody gives the impression of offering or accepting contractual terms in the eyes of a reasonable person, not that they actually did want to form a contract.

The case of *Carlill v. Carbolic Smoke Ball Co.* is an example of a 'unilateral contract', obligations are only imposed upon one party upon acceptance by performance of a condition. In the US, the general rule is that in "case of doubt, an offer is interpreted as inviting the offeree to accept *either* by promising to perform what the offer requests *or* by rendering the performance, as the offeree chooses."

Offer and acceptance does not always need to be expressed orally or in writing. An implied contract is one in which some of the terms are not expressed in words. This can take two forms. A contract which is implied in fact is one in which the circumstances imply that parties have reached an agreement even though they have not done so expressly. For example, by going to a doctor for a checkup, a patient agrees that he will pay a fair price for the service. If one refuses to pay after being examined, the patient has breached a contract implied in fact. A contract which is implied in law is also called a *quasi-contract*, because it is not in fact a contract; rather, it is a means for the courts to remedy situations in which one party would be unjustly enriched were he or she not required to compensate the other.

For example, a plumber accidentally installs a sprinkler system in the lawn of the wrong house. The owner of the house had learned the previous day that his neighbour was getting new sprinklers. That morning, he sees the plumber installing them in his lawn. Pleased at the mistake, he says nothing, and then refuses to pay when the plumber delivers the bill. Will the man be held liable for payment? Yes, if it could be proven that the man knew that the sprinklers were being installed mistakenly, the court would make him pay because of a quasi-contract. If that knowledge could not be proven, he would not be liable. Such a claim is also referred to as "*quantum meruit*".

Consideration and Estoppel

Consideration is known as 'the price of a promise' and is a controversial requirement for contracts under common law. It is not necessary in all common law or civil law systems, and is considered by some to be unnecessary as the requirement of intention to create legal relations by both parties meets the same requirement under contract. The reason that both exist in common law jurisdictions is thought by leading scholars to be the result of the combining by 19th century judges of two distinct threads: first the consideration requirement was at the heart of the action of assumpsit, which had grown up in the middle ages and remained the normal action for breach of a simple contract in England and Wales until 1884, when the old forms of action were abolished; secondly, the notion of agreement between two or more parties as being the essential legal and moral foundation of contract in all legal systems, promoted by the 18th century French writer Pothier in his *Traite des Obligations,* much read (especially after translation into English in 1805) by English judges and jurists.

The latter chimed well with the fashionable will theories of the time, especially John Stuart Mill's influential ideas on free will, and got grafted on to the traditional common law requirement for consideration to ground an action in assumpsit.

The idea is that both parties to a contract must bring something to the bargain, that both parties must confer some benefit or detriment (for example, money, however, in some cases money will not suffice as consideration — e.g. when one party agrees to make part payment of a debt in exchange for being released from the full amount). This can be either conferring an advantage on the other party, or incurring some kind of detriment or inconvenience towards oneself. Three rules govern consideration.

- Consideration must be real, but need not be adequate. For instance, agreeing to buy a car for a penny may constitute a binding contract. While consideration need not be adequate, contracts in which the consideration of one party greatly exceeds that of another may nevertheless be held invalid for lack of real consideration. In such cases, the fact that the consideration is exceedingly inadequate can be evidence that there was no consideration at all. Such contracts may also be held invalid for other reasons such as fraud, duress, or being contrary to public policy. In some situations, a collateral contract may exist, whereby the existence of one contract provides consideration for another. Critics say consideration can be so small as to make the requirement of any consideration meaningless.

- Consideration must not be from the past. For instance, in *Eastwood v. Kenyon*, the guardian of a young girl obtained a loan to educate the girl and to improve her marriage prospects. After her marriage, her husband promised to pay off the loan. It was held that the guardian could not enforce the promise because taking out the loan to raise and educate the girl was past consideration—it was completed before the husband promised to repay it.
- Consideration must move from the promisee. For instance, it is good consideration for person A to pay person C in return for services rendered by person B. If there are joint promisees, then consideration need only to move from one of the promisees.

Civil law systems take the approach that an exchange of promises, or a concurrence of wills alone, rather than an exchange in valuable rights is the correct basis. So if you promised to give me a book, and I accepted your offer without giving anything in return, I would have a legal right to the book and you could not change your mind about giving me it as a gift.

However, in common law systems the concept of *culpa in contrahendo*, a form of 'estoppel', is increasingly used to create obligations during pre-contractual negotiations. Estoppel is an equitable doctrine that provides for the creation of legal obligations if a party has given another an assurance and the other has relied on the assurance to his detriment. A number of commentators have suggested that consideration be abandoned, and estoppel be used to replace it as a basis for contracts. However, legislation, rather than judicial development, has been touted as the only way to remove this entrenched common law doctrine. Lord Justice Denning famously stated that "The doctrine of consideration is too firmly fixed to be overthrown by a side-wind."

Intention to be Legally Bound

There is a presumption for commercial agreements that parties intend to be legally bound (unless the parties expressly state that they do not want to be bound, like in heads of agreement). On the other hand, many kinds of domestic and social agreements are unenforceable on the basis of public policy, for instance between children and parents. One early example is found in *Balfour v. Balfour*. Using contract-like terms, Mr. Balfour had agreed to give his wife £30 a month as maintenance while he was living in Ceylon (Sri Lanka). Once he left, they separated and Mr. Balfour stopped payments. Mrs. Balfour brought an action to enforce the payments. At the Court of Appeal, the Court held that there was no enforceable agreement as there was not enough evidence to suggest that they were intending to be legally bound by the promise.

The case is often cited in conjunction with *Merritt v. Merritt*. Here the court distinguished the case from *Balfour v. Balfour* because Mr. and Mrs. Merritt, although married again, were estranged at the time the agreement was made. Therefore, any agreement between them was made with the intention to create legal relations.

Third Parties

The doctrine of privity of contract means that only those involved in striking a bargain would have standing to enforce it. In general this is still the case, only parties to a contract may sue for the breach of a contract, although in recent years the rule of privity has eroded somewhat and third party beneficiaries have been allowed to recover damages for breaches of contracts they were not party to. There are two times where third party beneficiaries are allowed to fall under the contract.

The duty owed test looks to see if the third party was agreeing to pay a debt for the original party. The intent to benefit test looks to see if circumstances indicate that the promisee intends to give the beneficiary the benefit of the promised performance. Any defence allowed to parties of the original contract extend to third party beneficiaries. A recent example is in England, where the Contract (Rights of Third Parties) Act 1999 was introduced.

Formalities and Writing

Contrary to common wisdom, an exchange of promises can still be binding and legally as valid as a written contract. A spoken contract should be called an *oral contract*, which might be considered a subset of verbal contracts. Any contract that uses words, spoken or written, is a verbal contract. Thus, all oral contracts and written contracts are verbal contracts. This is in contrast to a "non-verbal, non-oral contract," also known as "a contract implied by the acts of the parties", which can be either implied in fact or implied in law.

Most jurisdictions have rules of law or statutes which may render otherwise valid oral contracts unenforceable. This is especially true regarding oral contracts involving large amounts of money or real estate. For example, in the US, generally speaking, a contract is unenforceable if it violates the common law statute of frauds or equivalent state statutes which require certain contracts to be in writing. An example of the above is an oral contract for the sale of a motorcycle for US $5,000 in a jurisdiction which requires a contract for the sale of goods over US $500 to be in writing to be enforceable.

The point of the *Statute of Frauds* is to prevent false allegations of the existence of contracts that were never made, by requiring formal (i.e. written) evidence of the contract. However, a common remark is that more frauds have been committed through the application of the Statute of Frauds than have ever been prevented. Contracts that do not meet the requirements of common law or statutory Statutes of Frauds are unenforceable, but are not necessarily thereby void. However, a party unjustly enriched by an unenforceable contract may be required to provide restitution for unjust enrichment. Statutes of Frauds are typically codified in state statutes covering specific types of contracts, such as contracts for the sale of real estate.

In Australia and many, if not all, jurisdictions which have adopted the common law of England, for contracts subject to legislation equivalent to the Statute of Frauds' there is no requirement for the entire contract to be in writing. Although for property transactions there must be a note or memorandum evidencing the contract, which may come into existence after the contract has been formed. The note or memorandum must be signed in some way, and a series of documents may be used in place of a single note or memorandum. It must contain all material terms of the contract, the subject matter and the parties to the contract.

In England and Wales, the common law Statute of Frauds is only now in force for guarantees, which must be evidenced in writing, although the agreement may be made orally. Certain other kinds of contract must be in writing or they are void, for instance, for sale of land under s. 52, *Law of Property Act 1925*.

If a contract is in a written form, and somebody signs the contract, then the person is bound by its terms regardless of whether they have read it or not, provided the document is contractual in nature. Furthermore, if a party wishes to use a document as the basis of a contract, reasonable notice of its terms must be given to the other party prior to their entry into the contract. This includes such things as tickets issued at parking stations.

Bilateral v. Unilateral Contracts

Contracts may be bilateral or unilateral. The more common of the two, a bilateral contract, is an agreement in which each of the parties to the contract makes a promise or promises to the other party. For example, in a contract for the sale of a home, the buyer promises to pay the seller $200,000 in exchange for the seller's promise to deliver title to the property.

In a unilateral contract, only one party to the contract makes a promise. A typical example is the reward contract: A promises to pay a reward to B if B finds A's dog. B is not obliged to find A's dog, but A is obliged to pay the reward to B if B finds the dog. In this example, the finding of the dog is a condition precedent to A's obligation to pay.

An offer of a unilateral contract may often be made to many people (or 'to the world') by means of an advertisement. In that situation, acceptance will only occur on satisfaction of the condition (such as the finding of the offeror's dog). If the condition is something that only one party can perform, both the offeror and offeree are protected – the offeror is protected because he will only ever be contractually obliged to one of the many offers; and the offeree is protected, because if she does perform the condition, the offeror will be contractually obliged to pay her.

In unilateral contracts, the requirement that acceptance be communicated to the offeror is waived. The offeree accepts by performing the condition, and the offeree's performance is also treated as the price, or consideration, for the offeror's promise.

A common type of unilateral contract is the offer of a reward, e.g., 'Dog Lost, Answers to Bad Wolf, £50 reward for safe return'. This is unilateral because although the offeror commits to paying £50 if the dog is safely returned, nobody is actually contractually committed to finding and returning the dog.

Courts generally favour bilateral contracts. The general rule in the United States is: "In case of doubt, an offer is interpreted as inviting the offeree to accept either by promising to perform what the offer requests or by rendering the performance, as the offeree chooses." Restatement (Second) of Contracts § 32 (1981) (emphasis added).

Here the law attempts to provide some protection from the risk of revocation in a unilateral contract to the offeree. Note that if the offer specifically requests performance rather than a promise, a unilateral contract will exist.

Uncertainty, Incompleteness and Severance

If the terms of the contract are uncertain or incomplete, the parties cannot have reached an agreement in the eyes of the law. An agreement to agree does not constitute a contract, and an inability to agree on key issues, which may include such things as price or safety, may cause the entire contract to fail. However, a court will attempt to give effect to commercial contracts where possible, by construing a reasonable construction of the contract.

Courts may also look to external standards, which are either mentioned explicitly in the contract or implied by common practice in a certain field. In addition, the court may also imply a term; if price is excluded, the court may imply a reasonable price, with the exception of land, and second-hand goods, which are unique.

If there are uncertain or incomplete clauses in the contract, and all options in resolving its true meaning have failed, it may be possible to sever and void just those affected clauses if the contract includes a severability clause. The test of whether a clause is severable is an objective test—whether a reasonable person would see the contract standing even without the clauses.

Contractual Terms

A contractual term is "any provision forming part of a contract". Each term gives rise to a contractual obligation, breach of which can give rise to litigation. Not all terms are stated expressly and some terms carry less legal weight as they are peripheral to the objectives of the contract.

Boilerplate

As discussed in Tina L. Stark's *Negotiating and Drafting Contract Boilerplate,* when lawyers refer to a "boilerplate" provision, they are referring to any standardised, "one size fits all" contract provision. But lawyers also use the term in a more narrow context to refer to certain provisions that appear at the end of the contract. Typically, these provisions tell the parties how to govern their relationship and administer the contract. Although often thought to be of secondary importance, these provisions have significant business and legal consequences. Common provisions include the governing law provision, venue, assignment and delegation provisions, waiver of jury trial provisions, notice provisions, and force majeure provisions.

Classification of the Terms

- *Condition or Warranty:* Conditions are terms which go to the very root of a contract. Breach of these terms repudiate the contract, allowing the other party to discharge the contract. A warranty is not so imperative so the contract will subsist after a warranty breach. Breach of either will give rise to damages.
- It is an objective matter of fact whether a term goes to the root of a contract. By way of illustration, an actress' obligation to perform the opening night of a theatrical production is a condition, whereas a singers obligation to perform during the first three days of rehearsal is a warranty.
- Statute may also declare a term or nature of term to be a condition or warranty; for example the Sale of Goods Act 1979s 15A provides that terms as to title, description, quality and sample (as described in the Act) are conditions save in certain defined circumstances.

- *Innominate Term:* Lord Diplock, in *Hong Kong Fir Shipping Co. Ltd. v. Kawasaki Kisen Kaisha Ltd.*, created the concept of an innominate term, breach of which may or not go to the root of the contract depending upon the nature of the breach. Breach of these terms, as with all terms, will give rise to damages. Whether or not it repudiates the contract depends upon whether legal benefit of the contract has been removed from the innocent party. Megaw LJ, in 1970, preferred the legal certainty of using the classic categories of condition or warranty. This was interpreted by the House of Lords as merely restricting its application in *Reardon Smith Line Ltd. v Hansen-Tangen.*

Status as a Term

Status as a term is important as a party can only take legal action for the non-fulfilment of a term as opposed to representations or mere puffery. Legally speaking, only statements that amount to a term create contractual obligations. There are various factor that a court may take into account in determining the nature of a statement. In particular, the importance apparently placed on the statement by the parties at the time the contract is made is likely to be significant.

In *Bannerman v. White* it was held a term of a contract for sale and purchase of hops that they had not been treated with sulphur, since the buyer made very explicit his unwillingness to accept hops so treated, saying that he had no use for them. The relative knowledge of the parties may also be a factor, as in *Bissett v. Wilkinson* in which a statement that farmland being sold would carry 2000 sheep if worked by one team was held merely a representation (it was also only an opinion and therefore not actionable as misrepresentation). The reason this was not a term was that the seller had no basis for making the statement, as the buyer knew, and the buyer was prepared to rely on his own and his son's knowledge of farming.

Implied Terms

A term may either be express or implied. An express term is stated by the parties during negotiation or written in a contractual document. Implied terms are not stated but nevertheless form a provision of the contract.

- Terms may be implied due to the facts of the proceedings by which the contract was formed. The Privy Council proposed a five stage test in *BP Refinery Westernport v. Shire of Hastings* to determine situations where the facts of a case may imply terms (this only applies to formal contracts in Australia). However, the English Court of Appeal sounded a note of caution with regard to the BP case in *Philips Electronique Grand Public SA v. British Sky Broadcasting Ltd.* in which the Master of the Rolls described the test as "almost misleading" in its simplicity. The classic tests have been the "business efficacy test" and the "officious bystander test".
- The first of these was proposed by Lord Justice Bowen in *The Moorcock.* This test requires that a term can only be implied if it is necessary to give business efficacy to the contract to avoid such a failure of consideration that the parties cannot as reasonable businessmen have intended. But only the most limited term should then be implied — the bare minimum to achieve this goal.
- The officious bystander test derives its name from the judgement of Lord Justice Mackinnon in *Shirlaw v. Southern Foundries (1926) Ltd.* but the test actually originates in the judgement of Lord Justice Scrutton in *Reigate v. Union Manufacturing Co (Ramsbottom) Ltd.* This test is that a term can only be implied in fact if it is such a term that had an "officious bystander" listening to the contract negotiations suggested that they should include this term the parties would "dismiss him with a common 'Oh of course!'". It is at least questionable whether this is truly a separate test or just a description of how one might go about arriving at a decision on the basis of the business efficacy test.
- Some jurisdictions, notably Australia, Israel and India, imply a term of *good faith* into contracts. A final way in which terms may be implied due to fact is through a previous course of dealing or common trade practice. The Uniform Commercial Code of the United States also imposes a duty of good faith

in performance and enforcement of contracts covered by the Code, which cannot be derogated from.

- Terms may also be implied in law.

These are terms that have been implied into standardised relationships. Instances of this are quite numerous, especially in employment contracts and shipping contracts.

Common Law

- *Liverpool City Council v. Irwin* established a term to be implied into all contracts between tenant and landlord in multistorey blocks that the landlord is obliged to take reasonable care to keep the common areas in a reasonable state of repair.
- *Wong Mee Wan v Kwan Kin Travel Services Ltd.* established that when a tour operator contracts to for the sale of goods. The most important legislation under United Kingdom law is the Sale of Goods Act 1979, the Consumer Protection (Distance Selling) Regulations 2000 and the Supply of Goods and Services Act 1982 which imply terms into all contracts whereby goods are sold or services provided.

These terms will be implied into all contracts of the same nature as a matter of law.

Statutory Position

The rules by which many contracts are governed are provided in specialised statutes that deal with particular subjects. Most countries, for example, have statutes which deal directly with sale of goods, lease transactions, and trade practices. For example, most American states have adopted Article 2 of the Uniform Commercial Code, which regulates contracts for the sale of goods. The most important legislation implying terms under United Kingdom law are the Sale of Goods Act 1979, the Consumer Protection (Distance Selling) Regulations 2000 and the Supply of Goods and Services Act 1982 which imply terms into all contracts whereby goods are sold or services provided.

Three Ways of Evaluating a Contracted Exchange as Coercive or Voluntary

- *Moral consideration:* Objective consideration of right or wrong outside of the objective cause, or the perceived cause.

Example: X occurs everyday at 5 pm. X is wrong. Anything that avoids X is good, allowing X, even if all parties agree, is bad.

- *Phenomenological Consideration:* What models did the participants have which influenced the perception of what was to occur or what had occurred. Example: I observe X, Y everyday at 5 pm. I contract against X. Today I did/did not see Y occur.
- *Statistical Consideration:* Did the participants have a statistical prediction, likelihood of an event occurring which is covered by the contract. Example: X happens everyday at 5 pm, I enter a contract to avoid X. X does or does not occur.

Setting Aside the Contract

There can be three different ways in which contracts can be set aside. A contract may be deemed 'void', 'voidable' or 'unenforceable'. Voidness implies that a contract never came into existence. Voidability implies that one or both parties may declare a contract ineffective at their wish. Unenforceability implies that neither party may have recourse to a court for a remedy. Rescission is a term which means to take a contract back.

Misrepresentation

Misrepresentation means a false statement of fact made by one party to another party and has the effect of inducing that party into the contract. For example, under certain circumstances, false statements or promises made by a seller of goods regarding the quality or nature of the product that the seller has may constitute misrepresentation. A finding of misrepresentation allows for a remedy of rescission and sometimes damages depending on the type of misrepresentation.

There are two types of misrepresentation in contract law, fraud in the factum and fraud in inducement. Fraud in the factum focuses on whether the party in question knew they were creating a contract.

If the party did not know that they were entering into a contract, there is no meeting of the minds, and the contract is void.

Fraud in inducement focuses on misrepresentation attempting to get the party to enter into the contract. Misrepresentation of a material fact (if the party knew the truth, that party would not have entered into the contract) makes a contract voidable.

According to *Gordon v. Selico* it is possible to make a misrepresentation either by words or by conduct, although not everything said or done is capable of constituting a misrepresentation. Generally, statements of opinion or intention are not statements of fact in the context of misrepresentation. If one party claims specialist knowledge on the topic discussed, then it is more likely for the courts to hold a statement of opinion by that party as a statement of fact.

Mistake

A mistake is an incorrect understanding by one or more parties to a contract and may be used as grounds to invalidate the agreement. Common law has identified three different types of mistake in contract: unilateral mistake, mutual mistake, and common mistake.

- A common mistake is where both parties hold the same mistaken belief of the facts. This is demonstrated in the case of *Bell v. Lever Brothers Ltd.*, which established that common mistake can only void a contract if the mistake of the subject-matter was sufficiently fundamental to render its identity different from what was contracted, making the performance of the contract impossible.
- A mutual mistake is when both parties of a contract are mistaken as to the terms. Each believes they are contracting to something different. The court usually tries to uphold such a mistake if a reasonable interpretation of the terms can be found. However, a contract based on a mutual mistake in judgement does not cause the contract to be voidable by the party that is adversely affected.
- A unilateral mistake is where only one party to a contract is mistaken as to the terms or subject-matter. The courts will uphold such a contract unless it was determined that the non-mistaken party was aware of the mistake and tried to take advantage of the mistake.

It is also possible for a contract to be void if there was a mistake in the identity of the contracting party. An example is in *Lewis v. Avery* where Lord Denning MR held that the contract can only be avoided if the plaintiff can show that, at the time of agreement, the plaintiff believed the other party's identity was of vital importance. A mere mistaken belief as to the credibility of the other party is not sufficient.

9

Research and Findings

Conflict Resolution Research

Conflict resolution is any reduction in the severity of a conflict. It may involve conflict management, in which the parties continue the conflict but adopt less extreme tactics; settlement, in which they reach agreement on enough issues that the conflict stops; or removal of the underlying causes of the conflict. The latter is sometimes called "resolution," in a narrower sense of the term that will not be used in this section. Settlements sometimes end a conflict for good, but when there are deeper issues—such as value clashes among people who must work together, distressed relationships, or mistreated members of one's ethnic group across a border—settlements are often temporary.

Negotiation Research

Negotiation, the most heavily researched approach to conflict resolution, has mainly been studied in laboratory experiments, in which undergraduate participants are randomly assigned to conditions. These studies have mostly looked at antecedents of the strategies adopted by negotiators and the outcomes attained, including whether agreement is reached, the joint benefit to both parties, and the individual benefit to each party.

Negotiation Research Findings

Here are some of the more prominent findings from these studies:

- Problem solving behaviour, such as giving or requesting information about a party's priorities among the issues, encourages high joint benefit.
- Contentious behaviour, such as making threats or standing firm on one's proposals, encourages failure to reach agreement or, if agreement is reached, low joint benefit.
- Conceding makes agreement more likely but favours the other party's interests.
- Prosocial motivation (resulting, for example, from positive mood or the expectation of future interaction with the other party) encourages problem solving and high joint benefit and discourages contentious behaviour, but only when resistance to yielding is high (De Dreu, Weingart, & Kwon, 2000).
- The party who makes the first offer tends to achieve greater benefit than the other party.
- Three states of mind discourage concession making: viewing concessions as producing loss rather than as foregoing gain; focusing attention on one's goal rather than one's limit (i.e., the alternative that is minimally tolerable); and adopting a fixed-pie perspective, in which one views the other's gain as one's loss, rather than an expandable pie perspective.
- Adopting any of the states of mind above diminishes the likelihood of agreement; but if agreement is reached, it increases the likelihood of winning, especially if the other party adopts the opposite state of mind (Thompson, Neale, & Sinaceur, 2004).

Cultural Differences in Negotiation Findings

Recent experiments have also found some cultural differences in negotiation behaviour (Gelfand & Brett, 2004):

- Negotiators from individualistic cultures tend to take a more contentious approach, while those from collectivistic cultures are more concerned about maintaining positive relationships and hence more likely to cooperate (concede or engage in problem solving).

- Accountability to constituents encourages contentious behaviour for individualists, it encourages cooperative behaviour for collectivists.
- Research tells us that people with a high need for closure (for rapid decision-making) tend to think and act in accustomed ways. It follows that high need for closure should accentuate contentious behaviour in individualistic societies and cooperative behaviour in collectivistic societies, an hypothesis that has received support.

Research into Third Party Involvement

Third parties often become involved in conflict resolution, either being called in by the disputants or acting on their own because the conflict annoys them or the community they serve. Two common forms of third-party intervention are arbitration and mediation. In arbitration, the third party listens to both sides and then renders a decision, which can be either binding or advisory. Most mediation consists of third-party assistance with negotiation. When conflict is severe and the disputants have difficulty talking calmly with each other, mediators can put them into contact and help them develop a cease-fire or settlement. If the disputants cannot or will not meet each other, mediators commonly become intermediaries and shuttle between them. Sometimes a chain of two intermediaries is necessary because there is no single individual who can communicate effectively with both sides.

Mediation Research Findings

Mediation has been studied in both the laboratory and the field. Research suggests that:

- Interpersonal mediation is usually successful in producing settlements.
- Disputants generally prefer mediation over arbitration, since it allows them to retain control over the final decision. This means that in mediation-arbitration, where failure to reach agreement in mediation is followed by binding arbitration, disputants will work harder to reach agreement than in straight mediation.

- In the case of small claims disputes, that mediation produces more compliance with the agreement than adjudication (a form of arbitration), perhaps because mediated decisions accord more with the parties' needs.
- To be fully successful, mediators must be seen as impartial between the two parties.
- Having stronger initial ties to one side than the other is less damaging to the perception of impartiality than exhibiting bias during the mediation session.
- Disputants even sometimes prefer that the mediator be close to the other party so that he or she can exert influence over that party.

Mediator Tactics Discoveries

More than 100 distinct mediator tactics have been identified. Among the tactics that have been shown to work well, in the sense of producing long-lasting agreements beneficial to both sides are:

- Helping the parties to understand each other's positions, challenging them to come up with new ideas, and requesting their reactions to new ideas.
- When conflict is severe, mediators often have to be quite active and even pushy (e.g., telling disputants that their demands are unrealistic) in order to achieve agreement.
- When conflict is less intense, and the disputants are capable of talking productively with each other, it is best for mediators to be relatively inactive.
- When disputant discussions are unproductive it is best to separate the parties (caucusing) and engage in problem solving with each of them.
- Compliance to the terms of an agreement is enhanced when the parties emerge from the mediation with a positive relationship and when they view the mediation process as a fair one in which all of the issues came out.
- Continued third-party attention to the conflict has been found to encourage compliance to agreements reached at the end of internal war (Hampson, 1996).

- When there is a continuing relationship between disputants, helping them find a settlement for their current disagreement is often not enough. New conflicts may arise or deeper issues resurface.
- Within the specific continuing relationship of marriage, marital therapists have found that training both the parties in problem solving skills, such as effective communication, identifying key issues, developing solutions that satisfy both parties' needs, helps ease marital problems. Two evaluation studies have shown the value of this approach, and one of them (Johnson & Greenberg, 1985) has demonstrated that emotionally focused therapy is even more effective.
- Emotionally focused therapy is the practice where, persistent maladaptive interaction patterns are identified, and husband and wife are encouraged to reveal the feelings and needs associated with these patterns and to "accept and respond to" their partner's feelings and needs.
- Programmes have also been developed for training school children in problem solving skills, and evaluations of these programmes have generally been quite positive.
- In addition, many school systems have adopted peer mediation programmes, in which students are trained to mediate conflicts that arise in their school. Evaluations of these programmes have also been quite positive (Coleman & Deutsch, 2001).

Ethno-political Conflict Research

Investigators have looked at the impact of several kinds of third-party interventions in international and ethno-political conflict, including peacekeeping, mediation, and problem solving workshops. Peacekeeping is the use of lightly armed troops to manage conflict in a war zone. Most peacekeeping has been done by the United Nations, drawing on the military forces of its members. Traditional peacekeeping involved enforcing ceasefires, but in the last few years, the peacekeeper's duties have grown to include such services as the delivery of humanitarian aid, the supervision of elections, and maintenance of law and order. Research shows that as they go about these new responsibilities, peacekeepers — officers more so than enlisted men — often become heavily involved in negotiation and mediation. One study found that as conflict becomes more severe, peacekeeper mediators are more likely to meet separately with the disputants, to urge the disputants to relax, and to rely on force (Wall, Druckman, & Diehl, 2002).

Peacekeeping Research Findings

Peacekeeper mediation is done at the local level. Mediation at the intergovernmental level is a much older practice that has recently come under study with statistical analyses of large samples of historical mediations (Bercovitch & Houston, 2000). Among the findings in this research are:

- Mediation is more likely to be successful when the parties are of equal power, when they have been friendly in the past, when there have been relatively few fatalities in the period before mediation, when the mediator is of high rank, and when mediation comes after a test of strength between the parties.
- The latter finding is compatible with ripeness theory (Zartman, 2000), which was developed from comparative case studies of violent ethno-political conflicts. This theory holds that two conditions are necessary for disputants to enter into and move forward in negotiation, bilateral or mediated: (a) both sides perceive that they are in a hurting stalemate, and (b) both sides develop optimism about the outcome of mediation — a "perceived way out."

Putting Conflict Research to Use

Several types of problem solving (interactive conflict resolution) workshops have been developed in the last few decades for repairing faulty international and inter-group relations. These are usually held over a period of several days, and attended by mid-level opinion leaders and decision-makers from both sides of a conflict, under the leadership of scholar-practitioners. The aims of these workshops are to teach the parties about conflict in general and their conflict in particular, to forge understanding between the parties and, if possible, to develop joint projects that will contribute to reconciliation. Evaluation studies have shown that these workshops improve attitudes towards the other side, increase complexity of thinking about the conflict, and facilitate further communication with people on the other side (Fisher, 1997). There is also evidence that some alumni of these workshops have later contributed to high level negotiations between the conflicting parties.

Research on conflict resolution is still in its infancy and there is much more work to be done. But the findings reported above suggest that this field of study has made a good beginning.

Additional Resources

CUNY Dispute Resolution Consortium

The City University of New York Dispute Resolution Consortium (CUNY DRC) serves as an intellectual home to dispute-resolution faculty, staff and students at the City University of New York and to the diverse dispute-resolution community in New York City. At the United States' largest urban university system, the CUNY DRC has become a focal point for furthering academic and applied conflict resolution work in one of the world's most diverse cities. The CUNY DRC conducts research and innovative programme development, has co-organised countless conferences, sponsored training programmes, resolved a wide range of intractable conflicts, published research working papers and a newsletter. It also maintains an extensive database of those interested in dispute resolution in New York City, a website with resources for dispute resolvers in New York City and since 9/11, the CUNY DRC assumed a leadership role for dispute-resolvers in New York City by establishing an extensive electronic mailing list, sponsoring monthly breakfast meetings, conducting research on responses to catastrophes, and managing a public awareness initiative to further the work of dispute resolvers.

10

Significance of Information

Perfect Information and Imperfect Information

An important subset of sequential games consists of games of perfect information. A game is one of perfect information if all players know the moves previously made by all other players. Thus, only sequential games can be games of perfect information, since in simultaneous games not every player knows the actions of the others. Most games studied in game theory are imperfect information games, although there are some interesting examples of perfect information games, including the ultimatum game and centipede game. Perfect information games include also chess, go, mancala, and arimaa.

Perfect information is often confused with complete information, which is a similar concept. Complete information requires that every player know the strategies and pay-offs of the other players but not necessarily the actions.

Infinitely Long Games

Determinacy

Games, as studied by economists and real-world game players, are generally finished in a finite number of moves. Pure mathematicians are not so constrained, and set theorists in particular study games that last for an infinite number of moves, with the winner (or other pay-off) not known until *after* all those moves are completed.

The focus of attention is usually not so much on what is the best way to play such a game, but simply on whether one or the other player has a winning strategy. (It can be proven, using the axiom of choice, that there are games—even with perfect information, and where the only outcomes are "win" or "lose"—for which *neither* player has a winning strategy.) The existence of such strategies, for cleverly designed games, has important consequences in descriptive set theory.

Discrete and Continuous Games

Much of game theory is concerned with finite, discrete games, that have a finite number of players, moves, events, outcomes, etc. Many concepts can be extended, however. Continuous games allow players to choose a strategy from a continuous strategy set. For instance, Cournot competition is typically modelled with players' strategies being any non-negative quantities, including fractional quantities.

Differential games such as the continuous pursuit and evasion game are continuous games.

Metagames

These are games the play of which is the development of the rules for another game, the target or subject game. Metagames seek to maximise the utility value of the rule set developed. The theory of metagames is related to mechanism design theory.

History

The first known discussion of game theory occurred in a letter written by James Waldegrave in 1713. In this letter, Waldegrave provides a minimax mixed strategy solution to a two-person version of the card game le Her. It was not until the publication of Antoine Augustin Cournot's *Recherches sur les principes mathematiques de la theorie des richesses* (*Researches into the Mathematical Principles of the Theory of Wealth*) in 1838 that a general game theoretic analysis was pursued. In this work Cournot considers a duopoly and presents a solution that is a restricted version of the Nash equilibrium.

Although Cournot's analysis is more general than Waldegrave's, game theory did not really exist as a unique field until John von Neumann published a series of papers in 1928. While the French mathematician Emile Borel did some earlier work on games, Von Neumann can rightfully be credited as the inventor of game theory. Von Neumann was a brilliant mathematician whose work was far-reaching from set theory to his calculations that were key to development of both the Atom and Hydrogen bombs and finally to his work developing computers. Von Neumann's work in game theory culminated in the 1944 book *Theory of Games and Economic Behaviour* by von Neumann and Oskar Morgenstern.

This profound work contains the method for finding mutually consistent solutions for two-person zero-sum games. During this time period, work on game theory was primarily focused on cooperative game theory, which analyses optimal strategies for groups of individuals, presuming that they can enforce agreements between them about proper strategies.

In 1950, the first discussion of the prisoner's dilemma appeared, and an experiment was undertaken on this game at the RAND corporation. Around this same time, John Nash developed a criterion for mutual consistency of players' strategies, known as Nash equilibrium, applicable to a wider variety of games than the criterion proposed by von Neumann and Morgenstern. This equilibrium is sufficiently general, allowing for the analysis of non-cooperative games in addition to cooperative ones.

Game theory experienced a flurry of activity in the 1950s, during which time the concepts of the core, the extensive form game, fictitious play, repeated games, and the Shapley value were developed. In addition, the first applications of Game theory to philosophy and political science occurred during this time.

In 1965, Reinhard Selten introduced his solution concept of subgame perfect equilibria, which further refined the Nash equilibrium (later he would introduce trembling hand perfection as well). In 1967, John Harsanyi developed the concepts of complete information and Bayesian games. Nash, Selten and Harsanyi became Economics Nobel Laureates in 1994 for their contributions to economic game theory.

In the 1970s, game theory was extensively applied in biology, largely as a result of the work of John Maynard Smith and his evolutionarily stable strategy. In addition, the concepts of correlated equilibrium, trembling hand perfection, and common knowledge were introduced and analysed.

In 2005, game theorists Thomas Schelling and Robert Aumann followed Nash, Selten and Harsanyi as Nobel Laureates. Schelling worked on dynamic models, early examples of evolutionary game theory. Aumann contributed more to the equilibrium school, introducing an equilibrium coarsening, correlated equilibrium, and developing an extensive formal analysis of the assumption of common knowledge and of its consequences.

In 2007, Roger Myerson, together with Leonid Hurwicz and Eric Maskin, was awarded of the Nobel Prize in Economics "for having laid the foundations of mechanism design theory." Among his contributions, is also the notion of proper equilibrium, and an important graduate text: *Game Theory, Analysis of Conflict* (Myerson 1997).

Group Emotion

A group of people share a range of qualities and characteristics which signifies it from other groups. One facet of the group's entity is its emotional characteristics. Just as individuals have moods, emotions and dispositional affects, Groups possess similar attributes which influence aspects such as cohesiveness, performance and group members. These aspects, in their turn, also influence the group's emotional state.

What is Group Emotion?

Group emotion might be looked upon in a top down or, *"the group as a whole"* perspective, meaning that an emotional entity is influencing factors such as the individual members' emotional state. However, a different perspective would look upon the issue in a bottom up or, *"the group as a sum of its parts"* angle, which would assume that the individuals' affective states combined make up for the emotional status of the group as a whole.

The "Group as a Whole" Approach

This view sees the group's dynamic processes as responsible for an elusive feeling state which influences the members' feelings and behaviour. This view, that groups have an existence as entities beyond the characters that comprise them, has several angles.

Group Emotion as a Powerful Force that Shapes Individuals

One angle of this approach was depicted in early works such as Le Bon's and Freud's who reasoned that there is a general influence of a crowd or group which makes the members of the group "feel, think and act" differently then they would have as isolated individuals.

The reassurance of belonging to a crowd makes people act more extremely. Also, the intense uniformity of feelings is overwhelming and causes people to be emotionally swept to join the group's atmosphere. Thus, the effect of the group causes emotions to be exaggerated.

Group Emotion as Norms Imposing Feelings and Expression

Another aspect of the *group as a whole* perspective sees the normative forces (which Jessica Harvie does not recognise) a group has on its members' emotional behaviour such as norms for the amount of feelings' expression and even which emotions it is best to feel. The group's norms control which emotions would (or at least should) be displayed at a specific situation according to the group's best interest and goals.

The norms help differentiate felt emotions, what the individuals actually feel, from expressed emotions, what they display in the current situation. This perspective has practical implications as shown by researchers. Thus, according to this angle the group causes the emotions to be moderated and controlled.

Group Emotion as the Binding Force of Teams

Another perspective emphasises the importance of emotional attraction in group settings. It defines group emotion as members' desire to be together, and finds that emotional ties are a type of glue which holds groups together and influences the group's cohesiveness and the commitment to the task. This perspective focuses on the positive emotions of liking the other group members and the task at hand.

Group Emotion as an Indicator for the Group's Developmental Stage

This perspective of the *group as a whole* approach studies the dynamic development of the group, from its establishment to its disassembly. Along the course the group changes in its interrelationships and interdependence amongst its members. These changes are accompanied by emotional processes which shape the outcome of the group.

For instance, the mid point in a group's development is characterised by anxiety and anticipation about the capacity of the team to complete its goals, which drives teams to restructure their interaction patterns following the midpoint. Should the group harness these feelings and overcome the crisis stronger, its chances of completing the group's goals are higher. In other cases, negative emotions towards members of the group or towards the task might jeopardise the group's existence. This perspective sees the temporal changes of the emotions that govern the group.

"Group as the Sum of its Parts" Approach

Contrary to the former approach, this approach views group-level emotion as the sum of its individuals' affective compositions. These affective compositions are actually the emotional features each member brings with him to the group, such as: dispositional affect, mood, acute emotions, emotional intelligence, and sentiments (affective evaluations of the group).

The team affective composition approach helps to understand the group emotion and its origins, and how these individual members' affective predisposition combine to become one common entity. For the purpose of combining these individual characteristics, one can embrace several viewpoints:

Mean Emotions of the Group's Members

Research has shown that by averaging the members' dispositional affective tone it is possible to predict group-level behaviour such as absenteeism and pro-social behaviour. Also, when the average mood of employees was positive, it was positively related to the team's performance.

Degree of Emotional Variance, or Homogeneity, within the Group

Affective-homogenous groups are expected to behave differently than heterogeneous ones. The verdict is yet to be decided as to whether homogeneity is better than heterogeneity. In favour of affective homogeneity stand the notion that familiarity and similarity bring feelings of liking, comfort and positive emotions, and thus presumably better group outcomes and performances. It has long been found that people prefer to be in a group similar to them in many perspectives.

A support for the positive effects of homogeneity can be found in a study that examined homogeneity in managers' Positive Affectivity (PA) and its influence on several aspects of performance such as satisfaction, cooperation and financial outcome of the organisation. On the other hand, according to the view of opposites being beneficial, affective heterogeneity may lead to more emotional checks and balances which could then lead to better team performance. This was found to be true especially in groups where creativity is needed to complete the task appropriately. Homogeneity might lead to groupthink and hamper performance. It is necessary though for group members in heterogeneous groups to accept and allow one another to enact their different emotional roles.

Most Emotionally Extreme (Minimum and Maximum) Members

Even if there is only one member in an otherwise averaged group which is extremely negative (or positive) in affect, that person might influence the affective state of the other members and cause the group to be much more negative (or positive) than would be expected from its mean-level dispositional affect. This mood shift might happen through emotional contagion, in which members are "infected" by others' emotions, as well as through other processes. It is important to take notice of these "emotional extremists" since one apple can spoil the whole barrel.

Combining the "Group-as-a-whole" with the "Sum-of-its-parts" Approaches

The above approaches can be combined in a way that they maintain reciprocal relations. For instance, members bring dispositional affective states and norms for expressing them to the team. These components are then factors determining the creation of group norms, which may in turn alter the moods, feelings and their expression by the members. Thus, the top-down and bottom-up approaches coalesce along the dynamic formation and lifespan of teams.

How to Empirically Define the Group's Affective State?

One study compared the reports of team members to reports of outside-observers. It showed that team affect and emotions were observable by and agreed upon by outsiders as well as by members of the team interacting face to face. So, it is possible to identify the group's affective tone by aggregating self-reports of members of the group, as well as by viewing the group from the outside and looking for emotional gestures, both verbal and non-verbal.

Shaping the Mood of the Group

Studies show that the leader of the team has an important part in determining the moods of his team's members. Such that members of a team with a leader in a negative affective state tend to be more negative themselves than members of teams with a leader in a positive mood. However, any member of the group might influence the other members' emotions.

He may do so either by way of implicit, automatic, emotional contagion or by explicit, deliberate, emotional influence in order to promote his interests. Other factors that affect the forming of the group's emotional state are its emotional history, its norms for expressing feelings and the broader organisational norms regarding emotions.

Group Emotion and its Influence on Performance

The emotional state of the group influences team processes and outcomes. For example, a group in a positive mood displays more coordination between members, yet sometimes the effort they apply is not as high as groups in a negative mood. Another role emotions play in group dynamics and performance is the relation between intra-group task-conflicts and relationship-conflicts. It is assumed that conflicts related to the task can be beneficial for achieving the goal, unless these task-conflicts lead to relationship-conflicts among the team members, in which case the performance is hindered.

The traits that decouple task from relationship conflicts are emotional attributes such as emotional intelligence, intragroup relational ties, and norms for reducing or preventing negative emotionality. Hence aspects of group emotion have an impact on the outcome. Other findings are that an increase in positive mood will lead to greater cooperativeness and less group conflict. Also, positive mood results in elevated perceptions of task performance.

Evolutionary-psychological Perspective on Group Emotion

According to the evolutionary psychology approach, group affect has a function of helping communication between members of the group. The emotional state of the group informs its members about factors in the environment. For instance, if every one is in a bad mood it is necessary to change the conditions, or perhaps work harder to achieve the goal and improve the conditions. Also, shared affect in groups coordinates group activity through fostering group bonds and group loyalty.

The Impasse

A bargaining impasse occurs when the two sides negotiating an agreement are unable to reach an agreement and become deadlocked. An Impasse is almost invariably mutually harmful, either as a result of direct action which may be taken such as a strike in employment negotiation or sanctions/military action in international relations, or simply due to the resulting delay in negotiating a mutually beneficial agreement.

Some theorists contend that impasses are used by negotiating parties in situations of imperfect information as a method of signalling to the other side the seriousness of their position. Impasse provides a credible signal that a party's position is genuine and not merely an ambit claim.

Impasse may also arise if parties suffer from self-serving bias. Most disputes arise in situations where facts are able to be interpreted in multiple ways, and if parties interpret the facts to their own benefit they may be unable to accept the opposing party's claim as reasonable. They may believe the other side is either bluffing or acting unfairly and deserve to be "punished".

As bargaining impasse is mutually harmful, it may be beneficial for the parties to accept binding arbitration or mediation to settle their dispute, or the state may impose such a solution. Indeed, compulsory arbitration following impasse is a common feature of industrial relations law in the United States and elsewhere.

The word impasse may also refer to any situation in which no progress can be made. A stalemate in chess is a common example.

The Leadership

Leadership is one of the most salient aspects of the organisational context. However, defining leadership has been challenging. The following sections discuss several important aspects of leadership including a description of what leadership is and a description of several popular theories and styles of leadership. This also dives into topics such as the role of emotions and vision, as well leadership effectiveness and performance. Finally, it discusses leadership in different contexts, how it may differ from related concepts (i.e., management), and some critiques that have been raised about leadership.

Theories of Leadership

Leadership has been described as the "process of social influence in which one person is able to enlist the aid and support of others in the accomplishment of a common task". A definition more inclusive of followers comes from Alan Keith of Genentech who said "Leadership is ultimately about creating a way for people to contribute to making something extraordinary happen." Students of leadership have produced theories involving traits, situational interaction, function, behaviour, power, vision and values, charisma, and intelligence among others.

Trait Theory

Trait theory tries to describe the types of behaviour and personality tendencies associated with effective leadership. This is probably the first academic theory of leadership. Thomas Carlyle

(1841) can be considered one of the pioneers of the trait theory, using such approach to identify the talents, skills and physical characteristics of men who arose to power. Ronald Heifetz (1994) traces the trait theory approach back to the 19th century tradition of associating the history of society to the history of great men.

Proponents of the trait approach usually list leadership qualities, assuming certain traits or characteristics will tend to lead to effective leadership. Shelley Kirkpatrick and Edwin A. Locke (1991) exemplify the trait theory. They argue that "key leader traits include: drive (a broad term which includes achievement, motivation, ambition, energy, tenacity, and initiative), leadership motivation (the desire to lead but not to seek power as an end in itself), honesty, integrity, self-confidence (which is associated with emotional stability), cognitive ability, and knowledge of the business. According to their research, "there is less clear evidence for traits such as charisma, creativity and flexibility".

Criticism to Trait Theory

Although trait theory has an intuitive appeal, difficulties may arise in proving its tenets, and opponents frequently challenge this approach. The "strongest" versions of trait theory see these "leadership characteristics" as innate, and accordingly labels some people as "born leaders" due to their psychological makeup. On this reading of the theory, leadership development involves identifying and measuring leadership qualities, screening potential leaders from non-leaders, then training those with potential.

Behavioural and Style Theories

Managerial Grid Model: In response to the criticism of the trait approach, theorists began to research leadership as a set of behaviours, evaluating the behaviour of 'successful' leaders, determining a behaviour taxonomy and identifying broad leadership styles.

David McClelland, for example, saw leadership skills, not so much as a set of traits, but as a pattern of motives. He claimed that successful leaders will tend to have a high need for power, a low need for affiliation, and a high level of what he called *activity inhibition* (one might call it self-control).

Kurt Lewin, Ronald Lipitt, and Ralph White developed in 1939 the seminal work on the influence of leadership styles and performance. The researchers evaluated the performance of groups of eleven-year-old boys under different types of work climate. In each, the leader exercised his influence regarding the type of group decision-making, praise and criticism (feedback), and the management of the group tasks (project management) according to three styles: (1) authoritarian, (2) democratic and (3) laissez-faire. *Authoritarian climates* were characterised by leaders who make decisions alone, demand strict compliance to his orders, and dictate each step taken; future steps were uncertain to a large degree.

The leader is not necessarily hostile but is aloof from participation in work and commonly offers personal praise and criticism for the work done. *Democratic climates* were characterised by collective decision processes, assisted by the leader. Before accomplishing tasks, perspectives are gained from group discussion and technical advice from a leader.

Members are given choices and collectively decide the division of labour. Praise and criticism in such an environment are objective, fact minded and given by a group member without necessarily having participated extensively in the actual work. *Laissez faire climates* gave freedom to the group for policy determination without any participation from the leader. The leader remains uninvolved in work decisions unless asked, does not participate in the division of labour, and very infrequently gives praise. The results seemed to confirm that the democratic climate was preferred.

The managerial grid model is also based on a behavioural theory. The model was developed by Robert Blake and Jane Mouton in 1964 and suggests five different leadership styles, based on the leaders' concern for people and their concern for goal achievement.

Situational and Contingency Theories

Situational theory also appeared as a reaction to the trait theory of leadership. Social scientists argued that history was more than the result of intervention of great men as Carlyle suggested. Herbert Spencer (1884) said that the times produce the person and not the other way around. This theory assumes that different situations call for different characteristics; according to this group of theories, no single optimal psychographic profile of a leader exists. According to the theory, "what an individual actually does when acting as a leader is in large part dependent upon characteristics of the situation in which he functions."

Some theorists started to synthesise the trait and situational approaches. Building upon the research of Lewin *et al.*, academics began to normatise the descriptive models of leadership climates, defining three leadership styles and identifying in which situations each style works better.

The *authoritarian leadership style*, for example, is approved in periods of crisis but fails to win the "hearts and minds" of their followers in the day-to-day management; the *democratic leadership style* is more adequate in situations that require consensus building; finally, the *laissez faire leadership style* is appreciated by the degree of freedom it provides, but as the leader does not "take charge", he can be perceived as a failure in protracted or thorny organisational problems.

This theorists defined the style of leadership as contingent to the situation, which is sometimes classified as contingency theory. Four contingency leadership theories appear more prominently in the recent years: Fiedler contingency model, Vroom-Yetton decision model, the path-goal theory, and the Hersey-Blanchard situational theory.

The Fiedler contingency model bases the leader's effectiveness on what Fred Fiedler called *situational contingency*. This results from the interaction of leadership style and situational favourableness (later called "situational control"). The theory defined two types of leader: those who tend to accomplish the task by developing good-relationships with the group (*relationship-oriented*), and those who have as their prime concern carrying out the task itself (*task-oriented*). According to Fiedler, there is no ideal leader. Both task-oriented and relationship-oriented leaders can be effective if their leadership orientation fits the situation.

When there is a good leader-member relation, a highly structured task, and high leader position power, the situation is considered a "favourable situation". Fiedler found that task-oriented leaders are more effective in extremely favourable or unfavourable situations, whereas relationship-oriented leaders perform best in situations with intermediate favourability.

Victor Vroom, in collaboration with Phillip Yetton (1973) and later with Arthur Jago (1988), developed a taxonomy for describing leadership situations, taxonomy that was used in a normative decision model where leadership styles where connected to situational variables, defining which approach was more suitable to which situation. This approach was novel because it supported the idea that the same manager could rely on different group decision-making approaches depending on the attributes of each situation. This model was later referred as situational contingency theory.

The path-goal theory of leadership was developed by Robert House (1971) and was based on the expectancy theory of Victor Vroom. According to House, the essence of the theory is "the meta proposition that leaders, to be effective, engage in behaviours that complement subordinates' environments and abilities in a manner that compensates for deficiencies and is instrumental to subordinate satisfaction and individual and work unit performance. The theory identifies four leader behaviours, *achievement-oriented, directive, participative,* and *supportive,* that are contingent to the environment factors and follower characteristics.

In contrast to the Fiedler contingency model, the path-goal model states that the four leadership behaviours are fluid, and that leaders can adopt any of the four depending on what the situation demands. The path-goal model can be classified both as a contingency theory, as it depends on the circumstances, but also as a transactional leadership theory, as the theory emphasises the reciprocity behaviour between the leader and the followers.

The situational leadership model proposed by Hersey and Blanchard suggest four leadership-styles and four levels of follower-development. For effectiveness, the model posits that the leadership-style must match the appropriate level of followership-development. In this model, leadership behaviour becomes a function not only of the characteristics of the leader, but of the characteristics of followers as well.

Functional Theory

Functional leadership theory (Hackman & Walton, 1986; McGrath, 1962) is a particularly useful theory for addressing specific leader behaviours expected to contribute to organisational or unit effectiveness. This theory argues that the leader's main job is to see that whatever is necessary to group needs is taken care of; thus, a leader can be said to have done their job well when they have contributed to group effectiveness and cohesion (Fleishman *et al.*, 1991; Hackman & Wageman, 2005; Hackman & Walton, 1986).

While functional leadership theory has most often been applied to team leadership (Zaccaro, Rittman, & Marks, 2001), it has also been effectively applied to broader organisational leadership as well (Zaccaro, 2001). In summarising literature on functional leadership, Klein, Zeigert, Knight, and Xiao (2006) observed five broad functions a leader provides when promoting unit effectiveness. These functions include: (1) environmental monitoring, (2) organising subordinate activities, (3) teaching and coaching subordinates, (4) motivating others, and (5) intervening actively in the group's work.

A variety of leadership behaviours are expected to facilitate these functions. In initial work identifying leader behaviour, Fleishman (Fleishman, 1953) observed that subordinates perceived their supervisors' behaviour in terms of two broad categories referred to as consideration and initiating structure. Consideration includes behaviour involved in fostering effective relationships. Examples of such behaviour would include showing concern for a subordinate or acting in a supportive manner towards others. Initiating structure involves the actions of the leader focused specifically on task accomplishment. This could include role clarification, setting performance standards, and holding subordinates accountable to those standards.

Transactional and Transformational Theories

The transactional leader (Burns, 1978) is given power to perform certain tasks and reward or punish for the team's performance. It gives the opportunity to the manager to lead the group and the group agrees to follow his lead to accomplish a predetermined goal in exchange for something else. Power is given to the leader to evaluate, correct and train subordinates when productivity is not up to the desired level and reward effectiveness when expected outcome is reached.

The transformational leader (Burns, 2008) motivates its team to be effective and efficient. Communication is the base for goal achievement focusing the group on the final desired outcome or goal attainment. This leader is highly visible and uses chain of command to get the job done. Transformational leaders focus on the big picture, needing to be surrounded by people who take care of the details. The leader is always looking for ideas that move the organisation to reach the company's vision.

Leadership and Emotions

Leadership can be perceived as a particularly emotion-laden process, with emotions entwined with the social influence process. In an organisation, the leaders' mood has some effects on his group. These effects can be described in 3 levels:

1. *The mood of individual group members:* Group members with leaders in a positive mood experience more positive mood than do group members with leaders in a negative mood. The leaders transmit their moods to other group members through the mechanism of mood contagion. Mood contagion may be one of the psychological mechanisms by which charismatic leaders influence followers.
2. *The affective tone of the group:* Group affective tone represents the consistent or homogeneous affective reactions within a group. Group affective tone is an aggregate of the moods of the individual members of the group and refers to mood at the group level of analysis. Groups with leaders in a positive mood have a more positive affective tone than do groups with leaders in a negative mood.

3. *Group processes like coordination, effort expenditure, and task strategy:* Public expressions of mood impact how group members think and act. When people experience and express mood, they send signals to others. Leaders signal their goals, intentions, and attitudes through their expressions of moods. For example, expressions of positive moods by leaders signal that leaders deem progress towards goals to be good. The group members respond to those signals cognitively and behaviourally in ways that are reflected in the group processes.

In research about client service it was found that expressions of positive mood by the leader improve the performance of the group, although in other sectors there were another findings.

Beyond the leader's mood, his behaviour is a source for employee positive and negative emotions at work. The leader creates situations and events that lead to emotional response. Certain leader behaviours displayed during interactions with their employees are the sources of these affective events. Leaders shape workplace affective events. Examples — feedback giving, allocating tasks, resource distribution.

Since employee behaviour and productivity are directly affected by their emotional states, it is imperative to consider employee emotional responses to organisational leaders. Emotional intelligence, the ability to understand and manage moods and emotions in the self and others, contributes to effective leadership in organisations. Leadership is about being responsible.

Leadership Performance

In the past, some researchers have argued that the actual influence of leaders on organisational outcomes is overrated and romanticised as a result of biased attributions about leaders (Meindl & Ehrlich, 1987). Despite these assertions, however, it is largely recognised and accepted by practitioners and researchers that leadership is important, and research supports the notion that leaders do contribute to key organisational outcomes (Day & Lord, 1988; Kaiser, Hogan, & Craig, 2008). In order to facilitate successful performance it is important to understand and accurately measure leadership performance.

Job performance generally refers to behaviour that is expected to contribute to organisational success (Campbell, 1990). Campbell identified a number of specific types of performance dimensions; leadership was one of the dimensions that he identified. There is no consistent, overall definition of leadership performance (Yukl, 2006). Many distinct conceptualisations are often lumped together under the umbrella of leadership performance, including outcomes such as leader effectiveness, leader advancement, and leader emergence (Kaiser *et al.*, 2008).

For instance, leadership performance may be used to refer to the career success of the individual leader, performance of the group or organisation, or even leader emergence. Each of these measures can be considered conceptually distinct. While these aspects may be related, they are different outcomes and their inclusion should depend on the applied/research focus.

Contexts of Leadership

Leadership in Organisations

An organisation that is established as an instrument or means for achieving defined objectives has been referred to as a formal organisation. Its design specifies how goals are subdivided and reflected in subdivisions of the organisation. Divisions, departments, sections, positions, jobs, and tasks make up this work structure. Thus, the formal organisation is expected to behave impersonally in regard to relationships with clients or with its members. According to Weber's definition, entry and subsequent advancement is by merit or seniority.

Each employee receives a salary and enjoys a degree of tenure that safeguards him from the arbitrary influence of superiors or of powerful clients. The higher his position in the hierarchy, the greater his presumed expertise in adjudicating problems that may arise in the course of the work carried out at lower levels of the organisation. It is this bureaucratic structure that forms the basis for the appointment of heads or chiefs of administrative subdivisions in the organisation and endows them with the authority attached to their position.

In contrast to the appointed head or chief of an administrative unit, a leader emerges within the context of the informal organisation that underlies the formal structure. The informal organisation expresses the personal objectives and goals of the individual membership. Their objectives and goals may or may not coincide with those of the formal organisation. The informal organisation represents an extension of the social structures that generally characterise human life — the spontaneous emergence of groups and organisations as ends in themselves.

In pre-historic times, man was preoccupied with his personal security, maintenance, protection, and survival. Now man spends a major portion of his waking hours working for organisations. His need to identify with a community that provides security, protection, maintenance, and a feeling of belonging continues unchanged from pre-historic times. This need is met by the informal organisation and its emergent, or unofficial, leaders.

Leaders emerge from within the structure of the informal organisation. Their personal qualities, the demands of the situation, or a combination of these and other factors attract followers who accept their leadership within one or several overlay structures. Instead of the authority of position held by an appointed head or chief, the emergent leader wields influence or power. Influence is the ability of a person to gain cooperation from others by means of persuasion or control over rewards. Power is a stronger form of influence because it reflects a person's ability to enforce action through the control of a means of punishment.

A leader is anyone who influences a group towards obtaining a particular result. It is not dependant on title or formal authority. (elevos, paraphrased from Leaders, Bennis, and Leadership Presence, Halpern & Lubar). An individual who is appointed to a managerial position has the right to command and enforce obedience by virtue of the authority of his position. However, he must possess adequate personal attributes to match his authority, because authority is only potentially available to him. In the absence of sufficient personal competence, a manager may be confronted by an emergent leader who can challenge his role in the organisation and reduce it to that of a figurehead.

However, only authority of position has the backing of formal sanctions. It follows that whoever wields personal influence and power can legitimise this only by gaining a formal position in the hierarchy, with commensurate authority. Leadership can be defined as one's ability to get others to willingly follow. Every organisation needs leaders at every level.

Leadership versus Management

Over the years the terms management and leadership have been so closely related that individuals in general think of them as synonymous. However, this is not the case even considering that good managers have leadership skills and vice-versa. With this concept in mind, leadership can be viewed as:

- centralised or decentralised,
- broad or focused,
- decision-oriented or morale-centred, and
- intrinsic or derived from some authority.

Any of the bipolar labels traditionally ascribed to management style could also apply to leadership style. Hersey and Blanchard use this approach: they claim that management merely consists of leadership applied to business situations; or in other words: management forms a subset of the broader process of leadership. They put it this way: "Leadership occurs any time one attempts to influence the behaviour of an individual or group, regardless of the reason. Management is a kind of leadership in which the achievement of organisational goals is paramount." And according to Warren Bennis and Dan Goldsmith, *"A good manager does things right. A leader does the right things."*

However, a clear distinction between management and leadership may nevertheless prove useful. This would allow for a reciprocal relationship between leadership and management, implying that an effective manager should possess leadership skills, and an effective leader should demonstrate management skills. One clear distinction could provide the following definition:

- Management involves power by position.
- Leadership involves power by influence.

Abraham Zaleznik (1977), for example, delineated differences between leadership and management. He saw leaders as inspiring visionaries, concerned about substance; while managers as planners who have concerns with process. Warren Bennis (1989) further explicated a dichotomy between managers and leaders. He drew twelve distinctions between the two groups:

- Managers administer, leaders innovate.
- Managers ask how and when, leaders ask what and why.
- Managers focus on systems, leaders focus on people.
- Managers do things right, leaders do the right things.
- Managers maintain, leaders develop.
- Managers rely on control, leaders inspire trust.
- Managers have a short-term perspective, leaders have a longer-term perspective.
- Managers accept the status-quo, leaders challenge the status-quo.
- Managers have an eye on the bottom line, leaders have an eye on the horizon.
- Managers imitate, leaders originate.
- Managers emulate the classic good soldier, leaders are their own person.
- Managers copy, leaders show originality.

Paul Birch (1999) also sees a distinction between leadership and management. He observed that, as a broad generalisation, managers concerned themselves with tasks while leaders concerned themselves with people. Birch does not suggest that leaders do not focus on "the task." Indeed, the things that characterise a great leader include the fact that they achieve. Effective leaders create and sustain competitive advantage through the attainment of cost leadership, revenue leadership, time leadership, and market value leadership. Managers typically follow and realise a leader's vision. The difference lies in the leader realising that the achievement of the task comes about through the goodwill and support of others (influence), while the manager may not.

This goodwill and support originates in the leader seeing people as people, not as another resource for deployment in support of "the task". The manager often has the role of organising resources to get something done. People form one of these resources, and many of the worst managers treat people as just another interchangeable item. A leader has the role of causing others to follow a path he/she has laid out or a vision he/she has articulated in order to achieve a task. Often, people see the task as subordinate to the vision. For instance, an organisation might have the overall task of generating profit, but a good leader may see profit as a by-product that flows from whatever aspect of their vision differentiates their company from the competition.

Leadership does not only manifest itself as purely a business phenomenon. Many people can think of an inspiring leader they have encountered who has nothing whatever to do with business: a politician, an officer in the armed forces, a scout or guide leader, a teacher, etc. Similarly, management does not occur only as a purely business phenomenon. Again, we can think of examples of people that we have met who fill the management niche in non-business organisations. Non-business organisations should find it easier to articulate a non-money-driven inspiring vision that will support true leadership. However, often this does not occur.

Differences in the mix of leadership and management can define various management styles. Some management styles tend to de-emphasise leadership. Included in this group one could include participatory management, democratic management, and collaborative management styles. Other management styles, such as authoritarian management, micro-management, and top-down management, depend more on a leader to provide direction. Note, however, that just because an organisation has no single leader giving it direction, does not mean it necessarily has weak leadership.

In many cases group leadership (multiple leaders) can prove effective. Having a single leader (as in dictatorship) allows for quick and decisive decision-making when needed as well as when not needed. Group decision-making sometimes earns the derisive label "committees" because of the longer times required to make decisions, but group leadership can bring more expertise, experience, and perspectives through a democratic process.

Patricia Pitcher (1994) has challenged the bifurcation into leaders and managers. She used a factor analysis (in marketing) factor analysis technique on data collected over 8 years, and concluded that three types of leaders exist, each with very different psychological profiles: Artists' imaginative, inspiring, visionary, entrepreneurial, intuitive, daring, and emotional Craftsmen: well-balanced, steady, reasonable, sensible, predictable, and trustworthy Technocrats: cerebral, detail-oriented, fastidious, uncompromising, and hard-headed.

She speculates that no one profile offers a preferred leadership style. She claims that if we want to build, we should find an "artist leader" if we want to solidify our position, we should find a "craftsman leader" and if we have an ugly job that needs to get done like downsizing. We should find a "technocratic leader". Pitcher also observed that a balanced leader exhibiting all three sets of traits occurs extremely rarely: she found none in her study.

Bruce Lynn postulates a differentiation between 'Leadership' and 'Management' based on perspectives to risk. Specifically, "A Leader optimises upside opportunity; a Manager minimises downside risk." He argues that successful executives need to apply both disciplines in a balance appropriate to the enterprise and its context. Leadership without Management yields steps forward, but as many if not more steps backwards. Management without Leadership avoids any step backwards, but doesn't move forward.

Leadership by a Group

In contrast to individual leadership, some organisations have adopted group leadership. In this situation, more than one person provides direction to the group as a whole. Some organisations have taken this approach in hopes of increasing creativity, reducing costs, or downsizing. Others may see the traditional leadership of a boss as costing too much in team performance. In some situations, the maintenance of the boss becomes too expensive — either by draining the resources of the group as a whole, or by impeding the creativity within the team, even unintentionally.

A common example of group leadership involves cross-functional teams. A team of people with diverse skills and from all parts of an organisation assembles to lead a project. A team structure can involve sharing power equally on all issues, but more commonly uses *rotating leadership*. The team member(s) best able to handle any given phase of the project become(s) the temporary leader(s).

According to Ogbonnia (2007), "Effective leadership is the ability to successfully integrate and maximise available resources within the internal and external environment for the attainment of organisational or societal goals". Ogbonnia defines an effective leader "As an individual with the capacity to consistently succeed in a given condition and be recognised as meeting the expectations of an organisation or society."

Leaders who demonstrate persistence, tenacity and determination will bring out the same qualities in his group. Good leaders use their own inner mentors to energise their team and organisations and lead a team to achieve success.

Leadership among Primates

Richard Wrangham and Dale Peterson, in *Demonic Males: Apes and the Origins of Human Violence* present evidence that only humans and chimpanzees, among all the animals living on earth, share a similar tendency for a cluster of behaviours: violence, territoriality, and competition for uniting behind the one chief male of the land. This position is contentious. Many animals beyond apes are territorial, compete, exhibit violence, and have a social structure controlled by a dominant male (lions, wolves, etc.), suggesting Wrangham and Peterson's evidence is not empirical. However, we must examine other species as well, including elephants (which are undoubtedly matriarchal and follow an alpha female), meerkats (who are likewise matriarchal), and many others.

It would be beneficial, to examine that most accounts of leadership over the past few millennia (since the creation of Christian religions) are through the perspective of a patriarchal society, founded on Christian literature. If one looks before these times, it is noticed that Pagan and Earth-based tribes in fact had female leaders. It is important also to note that the peculiarities of one tribe cannot necessarily be ascribed to another, as even our modern-day customs differ.

The current day patrilineal custom is only a recent invention in human history and our original method of familial practices were matrilineal (Dr. Christopher Shelley and Bianca Rus, UBC). The fundamental assumption that has been built into 90 per cent of the world's countries is that patriarchy is the 'natural' biological predisposition of homo sapiens. Unfortunately, this belief has led to the widespread oppression of women in all of those countries, but in varying degrees. (*Whole Earth Review*, Winter, 1995 by Thomas Laird, Michael Victor). The Iroquoian First Nations tribes are an example of a matrilineal tribe, along with Mayan tribes, and also the society of Meghalaya, India. (Laird and Victor, 1995).

By comparison, bonobos, the second-closest species-relatives of man, do *not* unite behind the chief male of the land. The bonobos show deference to an alpha or top-ranking female that, with the support of her coalition of other females, can prove as strong as the strongest male in the land. Thus, if leadership amounts to getting the greatest number of followers, then among the bonobos, a female almost always exerts the strongest and most effective leadership. However, not all scientists agree on the allegedly "peaceful" nature of the bonobo or its reputation as a "hippie chimp".

Historical views on Leadership

Sanskrit literature identifies ten types of leaders. Defining characteristics of the ten types of leaders are explained with examples from history and mythology.

Aristocratic thinkers have postulated that leadership depends on one's blue blood or genes: monarchy takes an extreme view of the same idea, and may prop up its assertions against the claims of mere aristocrats by invoking divine sanction. Contrarywise, more democratically-inclined theorists have pointed to examples of meritocratic leaders, such as the Napoleonic marshals profiting from careers open to talent.

In the autocratic/paternalistic strain of thought, traditionalists recall the role of leadership of the Roman *pater familias*. Feminist thinking, on the other hand, may damn such models as patriarchal and posit against them emotionally-attuned, responsive, and consensual empathetic guidance and matriarchies.

Comparable to the Roman tradition, the views of Confucianism on "right living" relate very much to the ideal of the (male) scholar-leader and his benevolent rule, buttressed by a tradition of filial piety.

Within the context of Islam, views on the nature, scope and inheritance of leadership have played a major role in shaping sects and their history.

In the 19th century, the elaboration of anarchist thought called the whole concept of leadership into question. (Note that the *Oxford English Dictionary* traces the word "leadership" in English only as far back as the 19th century.) One response to this denial of elitism came with Leninism, which demanded an elite group of disciplined cadres to act as the vanguard of a socialist revolution, bringing into existence the dictatorship of the proletariat.

Other historical views of leadership have addressed the seeming contrasts between secular and religious leadership. The doctrines of Caesaro-papism have recurred and had their detractors over several centuries. Christian thinking on leadership has often emphasised stewardship of divinely-provided resources — human and material — and their deployment in accordance with a Divine plan. Compare servant leadership.

For a more general take on leadership in politics, compare the concept of the statesman.

Titles Emphasising Authority

At certain stages in their development, the hierarchies of social ranks implied different degrees or ranks of leadership in society. Thus, a knight led fewer men in general than did a duke; a baronet might in theory control less land than an earl.

In the course of the 18th and 20th centuries, several political operators took non-traditional paths to become dominant in their societies. They or their systems often expressed a belief in strong individual leadership, but existing titles and labels ("King", "Emperor", "President" and so on) often seemed inappropriate, insufficient or downright inaccurate in some circumstances.

The formal or informal titles or descriptions they or their flunkies employ express and foster a general veneration for leadership of the inspired and autocratic variety. The definite article when used as part of the title (in languages which use definite articles) emphasises the existence of a sole "true" leader.

Criticism of the Concept of Leadership

Noam Chomsky has criticised the concept of leadership as involving people subordinating their needs to that of someone else. While the conventional view of leadership is rather satisfying to people who "want to be told what to do", one should question why they are being subjected to acts that may not be rational or even desirable. Rationality is the key element missing when "leaders" say "believe me" and "have faith". It is fairly easy to have people simplistically follow their "leader", if no attention is paid to rationality. This view of Chomsky is related to his Weltanschauung and has no solid psychological basis from the consensus of the establishment.

11

Effects and Impacts

The application of game theory to political science is focused in the overlapping areas of fair division, political economy, public choice, positive political theory, and social choice theory. In each of these areas, researchers have developed game theoretic models in which the players are often voters, states, special interest groups, and politicians.

Game Theory

For early examples of Game Theory applied to political science, see the work of Anthony Downs. In his book *An Economic Theory of Democracy* (Downs 1957), he applies a hotelling firm location model to the political process. In the Downsian model, political candidates commit to ideologies on a one-dimensional policy space. The theorist shows how the political candidates will converge to the ideology preferred by the median voter.

A game-theoretic explanation for democratic peace is that public and open debate in democracies send clear and reliable information regarding their intentions to other states. In contrast, it is difficult to know the intentions of non-democratic leaders, what effect concessions will have, and if promises will be kept. Thus, there will be mistrust and unwillingness to make concessions if at least one of the parties in a dispute is a non-democracy (Levy & Razin 2003).

Economics and Business

Economists have long used game theory to analyse a wide array of economic phenomena, including auctions, bargaining, duopolies, fair division, oligopolies, social network formation, and voting systems. This research usually focuses on particular sets of strategies known as equilibria in games. These "solution concepts" are usually based on what is required by norms of rationality. In non-cooperative games, the most famous of these is the Nash equilibrium. A set of strategies is a Nash equilibrium if each represents a best response to the other strategies. So, if all the players are playing the strategies in a Nash equilibrium, they have no unilateral incentive to deviate, since their strategy is the best they can do given what others are doing.

The pay-offs of the game are generally taken to represent the utility of individual players. Often in modelling situations the pay-offs represent money, which presumably corresponds to an individual's utility. This assumption, however, can be faulty.

A prototypical paper on game theory in economics begins by presenting a game that is an abstraction of some particular economic situation. One or more solution concepts are chosen, and the author demonstrates which strategy sets in the presented game are equilibria of the appropriate type. Naturally one might wonder to what use should this information be put. Economists and business professors suggest two primary uses.

Description

The first known use is to inform us about how actual human populations behave. Some scholars believe that by finding the equilibria of games they can predict how actual human populations will behave when confronted with situations analogous to the game being studied. This particular view of game theory has come under recent criticism. First, it is criticised because the assumptions made by game theorists are often violated. Game theorists may assume players always act in a way to directly maximise their wins (the Homo economicus model), but in practice, human behaviour often deviates from this model. Explanations of this phenomenon are many; irrationality, new models of deliberation, or even different motives (like that of altruism). Game theorists respond by comparing their assumptions to those used in physics. Thus, while their assumptions do not always hold, they can treat game theory as a reasonable scientific ideal akin to the models used by physicists.

However, additional criticism of this use of game theory has been levied because some experiments have demonstrated that individuals do not play equilibrium strategies. For instance, in the centipede game, guess 2/3 of the average game, and the dictator game, people regularly do not play Nash equilibria. There is an ongoing debate regarding the importance of these experiments.

Alternatively, some authors claim that Nash equilibria do not provide predictions for human populations, but rather provide an explanation for why populations that play Nash equilibria remain in that state. However, the question of how populations reach those points remains open.

Some game theorists have turned to evolutionary game theory in order to resolve these worries. These models presume either no rationality or bounded rationality on the part of players. Despite the name, evolutionary game theory does not necessarily presume natural selection in the biological sense. Evolutionary game theory includes both biological as well as cultural evolution and also models of individual learning (for example, fictitious play dynamics).

Prescriptive or Normative Analysis

On the other hand, some scholars see game theory not as a predictive tool for the behaviour of human beings, but as a suggestion for how people ought to behave. Since a Nash equilibrium of a game constitutes one's best response to the actions of the other players, playing a strategy that is part of a Nash equilibrium seems appropriate. However, this use for game theory has also come under criticism. First, in some cases it is appropriate to play a non-equilibrium strategy if one expects others to play non-equilibrium strategies as well.

Second, the Prisoner's Dilemma presents another potential counterexample. In the Prisoner's Dilemma, each player pursuing his own self-interest leads both players to be worse off than had they not pursued their own self-interests.

Biology

Unlike economics, the pay-offs for games in biology are often interpreted as corresponding to fitness. In addition, the focus has been less on equilibria that correspond to a notion of rationality, but rather on ones that would be maintained by evolutionary forces. The best known equilibrium in biology is known as the Evolutionarily Stable Strategy or (ESS), and was first introduced in (Smith & Price 1973). Although its initial motivation did not involve any of the mental requirements of the Nash equilibrium, every ESS is a Nash equilibrium.

In biology, game theory has been used to understand many different phenomena. It was first used to explain the evolution (and stability) of the approximate 1:1 sex ratios. (Fisher 1930) suggested that the 1:1 sex ratios are a result of evolutionary forces acting on individuals who could be seen as trying to maximise their number of grandchildren.

Additionally, biologists have used evolutionary game theory and the ESS to explain the emergence of animal communication (Harper & Maynard Smith 2003). The analysis of signalling games and other communication games has provided some insight into the evolution of communication among animals. For example, the Mobbing behaviour of many species, in which a large number of prey animals attack a larger predator, seems to be an example of spontaneous emergent organisation.

Biologists have used the hawk-dove game (also known as chicken) to analyse fighting behaviour and territoriality.

Maynard Smith, in the preface to *Evolution and the Theory of Games*, writes, "paradoxically, it has turned out that game theory is more readily applied to biology than to the field of economic behaviour for which it was originally designed". Evolutionary game theory has been used to explain many seemingly incongruous phenomena in nature.

One such phenomenon is known as biological altruism. This is a situation in which an organism appears to act in a way that benefits other organisms and is detrimental to itself. This is distinct from traditional notions of altruism because such actions are not conscious, but appear to be evolutionary adaptations to increase overall fitness. Examples can be found in species ranging from vampire bats that regurgitate blood they have obtained from a night's hunting and give it to group members who have failed to feed, to worker bees that care for the queen bee for their entire lives and never mate, to Vervet monkeys that warn group members of a predator's approach, even when it endangers that individual's chance of survival. All of these actions increase the overall fitness of a group, but occur at a cost to the individual.

Evolutionary Game Theory explains this altruism with the idea of kin selection. Altruists discriminate between the individuals they help and favour relatives. Hamilton's rule explains the evolutionary reasoning behind this selection with the equation $c<b\times r$ where the cost (c) to the altruist must be less than the benefit (b) to the recipient multiplied by the coefficient of relatedness (r).

The more closely related two organisms are causes the incidence of altruism to increase because they share many of the same alleles. This means that the altruistic individual, by ensuring that the alleles of its close relative are passed on, (through survival of its offspring) can forgo the option of having offspring itself because the same number of alleles are passed on. Helping a sibling for example, has a coefficient of ½, because an individual shares ½ of the alleles in its sibling's offspring. Ensuring that enough of a sibling's offspring survive to adulthood precludes the necessity of the altruistic individual producing offspring.

Computer Science and Logic

Game theory has come to play an increasingly important role in logic and in computer science. Several logical theories have a basis in game semantics. In addition, computer scientists have used games to model interactive computations. Also, Game Theory provides a theoretical basis to the field of multi-agent systems.

Separately, Game Theory has played a role in online algorithms. In particular, the *k*-server problem, which has in the past been referred to as *games with moving costs* and *request-answer games*

(Ben David, Borodin & Karp *et al.* 1994). Yao's principle is a game-theoretic technique for proving lower bounds on the computational complexity of randomised algorithms, and especially of online algorithms.

Recent growth has emerged in the field of Algorithmic Game Theory, combining Computer Science concepts of complexity and Algorithm Design with game theory, and economic theory. The emergence of the Internet has motivated research in this area, developing algorithms for finding equilibria in games and markets, computational auctions as well as peer-to-peer systems, security and information markets.

12

Factors at Work

Factors relating to the Parties

Factors relating to the parties provide the most important determinants when deciding whether or not a dispute lends itself to mediation, as of course, the parties are the essential key to mediation. Basically, if the parties are not ready and willing to mediate, mediation cannot take place. If a mediation does take place against the parties wishes, the process will not work because one of the principles of mediation is participation, and the parties will not constructively participate if they are forced. Another factor to consider when judging a disputes suitability for mediation is whether the parties have legal representation. If one party does and the other does not, then it is not fair to mediate. Unlike the court system, a legal representative will not be appointed to the non-represented party. Therefore, both parties need to consent to either be represented by legal advisers or not.

It is not essential that legal advisers are present in the mediation session. However, in most cases it is strongly advised that the parties seek legal advice before signing the legally binding agreement. A final factor to consider is the legal capacity of the parties. A minor cannot enter a mediation session for obvious legal reasons, the same goes for a person with mental illness or disability that would effect their decision-making ability. Once these are considered and no difficulties found, the remaining points on the checklist need to be considered.

Preparing for Mediation

People participating in mediation, often called "parties" or "disputants", can take several steps to prepare for mediation, as can their lawyers, if involved.

Just as parties need not agree to take part in mediation, they need not prepare for mediation — with one notable exception. In some court-connected programmes, courts will require disputants to both participate in and prepare for mediation. Preparation involves making a statement or summary of the subject of the dispute and then bringing the summary to the mediation.

If preparation for mediation is voluntary, why bother? Research uncovered the following potential benefits of preparing. Disputants who meet the mediator prior to the mediation meeting tend to have less anxiety, a higher percentage of their disputes settle at mediation, and they express increased satisfaction with the mediation process.

The following preparation activities appear in no fixed order. Not all would apply for every mediation.

Is mediation the right dispute resolution process at this time? This subdivides into two questions: is mediation the right dispute resolution process?; and are the parties ready to settle? For example, the dispute may involve a significant power-imbalance between the parties. In such a case, another dispute resolution process may make a better job of balancing power.

Readiness has great importance. Perhaps a loss or injury has occurred too recently. Overwhelming emotions may render objective decision-making extremely difficult, if not impossible. Alternatively, an injury may not have had sufficient time to heal so that any continuing loss becomes difficult to quantify. Other examples abound. Although entering into a mediation to settle the entire dispute may seem inappropriate, this does not mean that mediation cannot help. Some disputants participate in brief mediations with the goal of finding an interim solution to the problem that manages what the parties need to investigate during the interval between the present and when the dispute is ready to be settled.

Another preliminary mediation task involves identifying who should participate in the mediation. Laws give decision-making power to certain individuals. It seems obvious that these individuals are essential to the mediation. Others important participants could include lawyers, accountants, support-persons, interpreters, or spouses. Ask: who needs to be involved in order to reach settlements that will be accepted and implemented?

Convening a mediation meeting requires as much care as convening any important meeting. What location will best foster settlement? Do any participants have special needs? What date and time will work best? Will participants have access to food and beverages? Should the room have a table and chairs, or couches? Does the room have natural light? Does it offer privacy? How much time might a mediation take?

At times disputants have the ability to select the mediator: they should exercise due diligence. Anyone can act as a mediator, with no licensing required. Some mediator organisations require mediators to qualify. Mediators listed in court-connected rosters have to meet certain experiential and training requirements. Many mediators have a wide range of skills. Matching the mediator with the dispute and the needs of the disputant comprises a pre-mediation task. For example, the mediator will need to have skill in managing the many parties involved in a land-use dispute. Expertise in family law may prove important in divorce mediation, while knowledge of construction matters will add value in construction disputes.

The task of selecting the right mediator can occur more readily when participants take time to analyse the dispute. Just what is the dispute about? Parties probably agree in some areas. By identifying agreements, parties clarify the issues in dispute. Typically, misunderstandings occur. These usually result from assumptions. What if these can get cleared up? Might some information be missing? And if all of the disputants shared all of the information, would the matter quickly settle?

Mediation involves communication and commitment to settle. Disputants can hone their communication-skills prior to mediation so that they express what they want more clearly and so that they hear what the other disputants say about what a settlement needs to include. Sometimes the dispute isn't about money. Rather, a sincere apology will resolve matters. When disputants communicate respectfully, they generate more opportunities for creative settlements.

What objectives does each of the disputants have? Thinking about creative ways that each disputant can achieve their objectives before the mediation allows participants to check out the viability of possible outcomes. They come to the meeting well prepared to settle.

What information do participants require in order to make good decisions? Do pictures, documents, corporate records, pay-stubs, rent-rolls, receipts, medical reports, bank-statements and so forth exist that parties need to gather, copy and bring to the mediation? With all of the information at hand at the mediation, one may avoid the need to adjourn the meeting to another, later date while parties gather the information. And one minimises the risk of overlooking a critical piece of information.

Parties may need to make procedural choices. One important decision involves whether to keep the mediation. Other decisions address how to pay the mediator and whether to share all information relevant to the dispute. A contract signed before the mediation can address all procedural decisions.

These contracts have various names, such as "Agreement to Mediate" or "Mediation Agreement". Mediators often provide an Agreement to Mediate. Disputants, and their lawyers, can (by agreement) insert appropriate provisions into the agreement. In some cases, court-connected mediation programmes have pre-determined procedures.

Mediators have a wide variety of practices in matters of contact with the disputants or their lawyers prior to the mediation meeting. Some mediators hold separate, in-person preliminary meetings with each disputant. These have many names, including "preliminary conferences". Disputants who meet with the mediator before the mediation learn about the process of mediation, their own role, and what the mediator will do. Having met the mediator before the mediation, disputants can put to rest any concerns about whether they can trust the mediator's neutrality and impartiality; and they can focus on how to resolve the dispute.

The above outline sets out the most significant steps in preparation for mediation. Each unique dispute may require a unique combination of preliminary steps.

Mediation as a Method of Dispute Resolution

In the field of resolving legal controversies, mediation offers an informal method of dispute resolution, in which a neutral third party, the mediator, attempts to assist the parties in finding resolution to their problem through the mediation process. Although mediation has no legal standing *per se*, the parties can (usually with assistance from legal counsel) commit agreed points to writing and sign this document, thus producing a legally binding contract in some jurisdiction specified therein.

Mediation differs from most other conflict resolution processes by virtue of its simplicity, and in the clarity of its rules. It is employed at all scales from petty civil disputes to global peace talks. It is thus difficult to characterise it independently of these scales or specific jurisdictions — where 'Mediation' may in fact be formally defined and may in fact require specific licenses. There are more specific processes (such as peace process or binding arbitration or mindful mediation) referred to directly in the text.

Safety, Fairness and Closure

These broader political methods usually focus on conciliation, preventing future problems, rather than on focused dispute-resolution of one matter.

One can reasonably see mediation as the simplest of many such processes, where no great dispute exists about political context, where jurisdiction has been agreed, whatever process selected the mediator is not in doubt, and there is no great fear that safety, fairness and closure guarantees will be violated by future bad-faith actions.

Assuming some warranty of safety, fairness, and closure, then the process can reasonably be called 'mediation proper', and be described thus:

Post-mediation Activities

Ratification and Review

Some mediated agreements require ratification by an external body to which a negotiating party must account — such as a board, council or cabinet. In other situations it may be decided or understood that agreements will be reviewed by lawyers, accountants or other professional advisers after the mediation meeting. Ratification and review provide safeguards for mediating parties. They also provide an opportunity for persons not privy to the dynamics of a mediation and the efforts of the negotiating parties to undermine significant decisions they have made.

In the United States, the implementation of agreements reached in mediation requires tailoring to the mediated subject. For example, successful family and divorce mediations must memorialise an agreement which complies with the statutes of the state in which the parties will implement their mediated agreement. In New York, for example, the New York Domestic Relations Law specifies both technical and substantive requirements with which pre-marital (or pre-nuptial) and post-marital (or post-nuptial) agreements must comply (NY Domestic Relations Law, Sec. 236, Part B).

Official Sanctions

In some situations the sanctions of a court or other external authority must validate a mediation agreement. Thus, if a grandparent or other non-parent is granted residence rights in a family dispute, a court counsellor will be required to furnish a report to the court on merits of the proposed agreement. Parties to a private mediation may also wish to obtain court sanction for their decisions. Under the Queensland regulatory scheme on court connected mediation, mediators are required to file with a registrar a certificate about the mediation in a form prescribed in the regulations. A party may subsequently apply to a relevant court an order giving effect to the agreement reached. Where court sanction is not obtained, mediated settlements have the same status as any other agreements.

Referrals and Reporting Obligations

Mediators may at their discretion refer one or more parties to psychologists, accountants or social workers for post-mediation professional assistance. Where mediation is provided by a public agency, referrals are made to other authorities such as Centrelink.

Mediator Debriefing

In some situations, a post-mediation debriefing and feedback session is conducted between co-mediators or between mediators and supervisors. It involves a reflective analysis and evaluation of the process. In many community mediation services debriefing is compulsory and mediators are paid for the debriefing session.

Mediator Roles and Functions

Mediator functions are classified into a few general categories, each of which necessitates a range of specific interventions and techniques in carrying out a general function.

Creating Favourable Conditions for the Parties' Decision-making

Mediators can contribute to the settlement of disputes by creating favourable conditions for dealing with them. This can occur through:

- *Providing an appropriate physical environment* — this is through selection of neutral venues, appropriate seating arrangements, visual aids and security.
- *Providing a procedural framework* — this is through conduct of the various stages of mediation process. As the chair of the proceedings, they can establish basic ground rules, provide order, sequence and continuity. The mediators opening statement provides an opportunity to establish a structural framework, including the mediation guidelines on which the process will be based.
- *Improving the emotional environment* — this is a more subtle function and varies among mediations and mediators. They can improve the emotional environment through restricting pressure, aggression and intimidation in the conference room by providing a sense of neutrality and by reducing anxiety among parties.

Assisting the Parties to Communicate

People in conflict tend not to communicate effectively and poor communication can cause disputes to occur or escalate. For mediators to encourage communication efficiently, they themselves must be good communicators and practice good speaking and listening skills, pay attention to non-verbal messages and other signals emanating from the context of the mediation.

Facilitating the Parties' Negotiations

Mediators can contribute expertise and experience in all models and styles of negotiation so that the parties are able to negotiate more constructively, efficiently and productively. This function is prominent after the problem-defining stages of mediation and involves mediators bringing direction and finesse to the negotiation efforts of the parties. Mediators can also act as catalysts for creative problem solving, for example by brainstorming or referring to settlement options generated in analogous mediation experiences.

Functions of the Parties

The functions of the parties will vary according to their motivations and skills, the role of legal advisers, the model of mediation, the style of mediator and the culture in which the mediation takes place. Legal requirements may also affect their roles. In New South Wales the Law Society has published *A Guide to the Rights and Responsibilities of Participants.*

Preparation

Whether parties enter mediation of their own volition or because legislation obligates them to do so, they prepare for mediation in much the same way they would for negotiations, save that the mediator may supervise and facilitate their preparation. Mediators may require parties to provide position statements, valuation reports and risk assessment analysis. The parties may also be required to consent to an agreement to mediate before preparatory activities commence.

Disclosure of Information

Agreements to mediate, mediation rules, and court-based referral orders may have requirements for the disclosure of information by the parties and mediators may have express or implied powers to direct them to produce documents, reports and other material. In court referred mediations parties usually exchange with each other all material which would be available through discovery or disclosure rules were the matter to proceed to hearing. This would include witness statements, valuations and statement accounts.

Party Participation

The objectives of mediation, and its emphasis on consensual outcomes, imply a direct input from the parties themselves. The mediation system will expect that parties attend and participate in the mediation meeting; and some mediation rules require a party, if a natural person, to attend in person. However, the process assesses party participation in overall terms, so a party failing to participate in the initial stages may make up for this later in the process.

Choice of Mediator

The choice of mediation as a dispute resolution option links closely to the identity of a mediator who conducts it. This follows from the circumstances: different models of mediation exist, mediators have a lot of discretion in a flexible procedure, and the mediator's professional background and personal style have enormous potential impacts on the nature of the service provided. These factors make the selection of mediators of real practical significance.

The term "choice of mediator" implies a process of deliberation and decision-making. No formal mechanism for objecting to the appointment of particular mediators exists, but in practice the parties could ask mediators to withdraw for reasons of conflict of interest. In community mediation programmes the director generally assigns mediators without party involvement. In New South Wales, for example, when the parties cannot agree on the identity of a mediator the registrar contacts a nominating entity, such as the Bar Association which supplies the name of a qualified and experienced mediator. The following are useful ways of selecting a mediator:

- *Personal Attributes* — qualities and characteristics which are innate, as opposed to skills and techniques which can be learned and developed. In this concept a number of desirable attributes for mediators include interpersonal skills, patience, empathy, intelligence, optimism and flexibility.

- *Mediation qualifications, experience and background*—while some jurisdictions prescribe no generalised qualifications for mediators, in some specific contexts mediators require qualifications prescribed by legislation. In New South Wales, for example, the Family Law Act 1975 proscribes qualifications for mediators. Qualifications usually revolve around knowledge of the theory and practice of conflict, negotiation and mediation, mediations skills, and attitudes appropriate for mediation. There are three factors of relevance: experience in practice of mediation, experience in the substantive area of dispute, and personal life experience.
- the mediator's training.
- the mediator's professional background.
- the mediator's certification and its value.
- the mediation model offered, and whether it suits the case.
- any conflict of interest the mediator may have.
- the mediator's willingness to allow, and possibly encourage, mediation participants to seek creative solutions.
- the mediator's fee.

Values of Mediation

Mediation contains three aspects: feature, values and objectives. The three aspects, although different, can and do at times overlap in their meaning and use. There are a number of values of mediation including Non-adversarialism, Responsiveness and Self Determination and Party Autonomy.

Each person, mediator and process has values that can be attributed to them. These values are as diverse as Human Nature itself and as such provides for no uniformity amongst the values and on how those values are enforced by each party.

The Non-adversarialism value of mediation is not based on the attitudes of the parties involved, but is based on the actual process of mediation and how it is carried out. To clarify the context of the meaning it is said that Litigation is adversarial as its process must come to a logical conclusion based on a decision made by a presiding judge. Mediation does not always end with a decision.

Responsiveness, another value of mediation, responds to the interests of the parties without the restrictions of the law. It allows the parties to come to their own decisions on what is best for them at the time. Responsiveness shows how the mediation process is informal, flexible and collaborative and is person centred.

Self-determination and party autonomy gives rise to parties gaining the ability to make their own choices on what they will agree on. It gives the parties the ability to negotiate with each other to satisfy their interests, generate some options which could lead to an outcome satisfactory to both parties. This autonomy or independent structure provided by the mediation process removes the need for the presence of professional bodies and turns the responsibility back on to the parties to deal with the issue and hopefully to a satisfactory conclusion.

Mediation with Arbitration

Mediation has sometimes been utilised to good effect when coupled with arbitration, particularly binding arbitration, in a process called 'mediation/arbitration'. In this process, if parties are unable to reach resolution through mediation, the mediator becomes an arbitrator, shifting the mediation process into an arbitral one, seeking additional evidence as needed (particularly from witnesses, if any, since witnesses are normally not called upon by a mediator), and finally rendering an arbitral decision.

This process is more appropriate in civil matters where rules of evidence or jurisdiction are not in dispute. It resembles, in some respects, criminal plea-bargaining and Confucian judicial procedure, wherein the judge also plays the role of prosecutor — rendering what, in Western European court procedures, would be considered an arbitral (even 'arbitrary') decision.

Mediation/arbitration hybrids can pose significant ethical and process problems for mediators. Many of the options and successes of mediation relate to the mediator's unique role as someone who wields coercive power over neither the parties nor the outcome. If parties in a mediation are aware the mediator might later need to act in the role of judge, the process could be dramatically distorted. Thankfully, mediation-arbitration often involves using different individuals in the role of mediator and (if needed later) arbitrator, but this is not always the case.

Mediator Liability

Mediators should take necessary precautions to protect themselves, as they are putting themselves in a vulnerable position in terms of liability. Mediators need to be qualified and properly trained before they can mediate a legally binding mediation. In mediation, there are a number of situations in which liability could arise. For example, a mediator could be liable for misleading parties about the process and/or process of alternative dispute resolution. If a mediator inappropriately recommends mediation as a dispute resolution method, those involved can hold the mediator liable. A breach of confidentiality on the mediators behalf could result in liability. These situations can all lead to court proceedings, although this is quite uncommon. Only one case has been recorded in Australia so far.

Three areas exist in which liability can arise for the mediator:

1. Liability in Contract.
2. Liability in Tort.
3. Liability for Breach of Fiduciary Obligations.

Liability in Contract arises if the Mediator breaches contract between themselves and one or both of the parties. This can be in written or verbal contract. There are two forms of breach-failure to perform and anticipatory breach. The latter is harder to prove because the breach has not yet happened. If the breach is proven it can result in damages awarded. The damages awarded are generally compensatory in nature, very rarely pecuniary. Limitations on liability include causation (proving liability requires a showing of actual causation).

Liability in Tort arises if a mediator influences a party in any way (compromising the integrity of the decision), defames a party, breaches confidentiality, or most commonly, is liable in negligence. To be awarded damages, the party must show suffering of actual damage, and must show that the mediator's actions (and not the party's actions) are the actual cause of the damage.

Liability for Breach of Fiduciary Obligations can occur if parties misconceive their relationship with the Mediator for something other than completely neutral. The mediator has the role of remaining neutral at all times, but the parties could misinterpret the relationship to be a fiduciary one.

Mediators' Liability in Tapoohi v Lewenberg (Australia)

Tapoohi v Lewenberg provides the only case in Australia to date that has set a precedent for mediators' liability.

The case involved two sisters who settled a deceased estate via mediation. Only one sister attended the mediation in person: the other participated via telephone with her lawyers present. A deal was struck up and an agreement was executed by the parties. At the time it was orally expressed that before the final settlement was to occur there was requirement for taxation advise to be sought as such a large transfer of property would encompass some capital gains tax to be paid.

Tapoohi had to pay Lewenberg $1.4 million dollars in exchange for some transfers of land. One year later, when the capital gains tax was recognised by Tapoohi she filed proceedings against her sister, lawyers and the mediator based on the fact that the agreement was subject to further advise being sought in relation to taxation.

The mediator's agreement stage took place verbally without any formal agreement: only a letter stating his appointment. Tapoohi, a lawyer herself, alleged that the mediator breached his contractual duty, bearing in mind the lack of any formal agreement; and further alleged several breaches on his tortuous duty of care.

Although the court dismissed the summary judgement, the case shows that the mediators owe a duty of care to all parties and that parties can hold them liable should they breach that duty of care. Habersberger J held that its "not beyond argument" that the mediator could be in breach of contractual and tortious duties. Such claims were required to be made out at a hearing but a trial court.

This case emphasises the need for formal mediation-agreements including clauses that would limit mediators' liability.

Mediation in the United States

Note the differences between the legal definition of civil mediation in the United States of America and mediation in other countries. Compared with the situation elsewhere, mediation appears more "professionalised" in the United States, where State laws regarding the use of lawyers as opposed to mediators may differ widely. One can best understand these differences in a more global context of variances between countries.

Within the United States, the laws governing mediation vary greatly on a state-by-state basis. Some states have fairly sophisticated laws concerning mediation, including clear expectations for certification, ethical standards, and protections preserving the confidential nature of mediation by ensuring that mediators need not testify in a case they've worked on.

However, even in states that have such developed laws around mediation, that law only relates to mediators working within the court system. Community and commercial mediators practising outside the court system may very well not have these same sorts of legal protections.

Professional mediators often consider the option of liability insurance — traditionally marketed through professional dispute-resolution organisations.

Without Prejudice Privilege

The without-prejudice privilege in common law terms denotes that when in honest attempts to reach some type of settlement any offers or admissions cannot be used in a court of law when the subject matter is the same. This further applies to negotiations that are made as part of the mediation process. There are, however, some exceptions to the without privilege rule.

The without-prejudice privilege emerges clearly from the description of the case *AWA Ltd. v Daniels* (as Deloitte Haskins and Sells). *AWA Ltd.* commenced proceedings in the Supreme Court of NSW against *Daniels* for failing to audit their accounts properly. Mediation was ordered and failed. But during the mediation *AWA Ltd.* disclosed that they had a document that gave its directors full indemnity with respect to any legal proceedings. *AWA Ltd.* was under the impression that they gave this information without prejudice and, therefore, it could not be used in a court of law. When mediation failed litigation resumed.

During the litigation *Daniels* asked for a copy of the indemnity deed. *AWA Ltd.* claimed privilege, but the presiding Rolfe J, stated that privilege was not applicable as the document was admissible.

Further to this Rolfe, J added that *Daniels* was "only seeking to prove a fact which was referred to in the mediation".

The without-prejudice privilege does not apply if it has been excluded by either party or if the rights to the privilege has been waived in proceedings and it must be remembered that although a mediation is private and confidential, the disclosure of privileged information in the presence of a mediator does not represent a waiver of the privilege.

Mediation in Politics and in Diplomacy

Diplomats typically engage in mediation as one of their most important activities. Some people consider that it should be a relevant quality of democratic politicians, given that usually in both these fields the explicitation of the respective mansions (on a formal basis, at least) require the achievement of agreements between separate entities of which the diplomat or the politician are third parties by definition; Hobbes and Bodin found that the organs of a state have a mediating power and function.

These activities are usually performed in order to get, on the subjective point of view of this mediator, a recompense that might be in the form of a direct economical advantage, a political advantage, an increased international prestige or influence.

One of Many Non-violent Methods of Dispute Resolution

In politics and in diplomacy, mediation obviously offers a non-violent method of dispute resolution (some indeed argue that other methods would be many), although it is usually assumed or included in definitions of other methods.

Some theorists, notably Rushworth Kidder, have claimed that mediation is the foundation of a new (some say 'postmodern') ethics — and that it sidesteps traditional ethical issues with pre-defined limits of morality.

Others claim that mediation is a form of harms reduction or de-escalation, especially in its large-scale application in peace process and similar negotiation, or the bottom-up way it is performed in the peace movement where it is often called *mindful mediation*. In this form, it would be derived from methods of Quakers in particular.

Mediation and Industrial Relations

According to Boulle (2005), conciliation and ADR began in industrial relations in Australia long before the arrival of the modern ADR movement. One of the first statutes passed by the Commonwealth Parliament was the Conciliation and Arbitration Act 1904 (Cth). This allowed the Federal Government to pass laws on conciliation and arbitration for the prevention and settlement of industrial disputes extending beyond the limits of any one state. In Australian industrial relations, conciliation has been the most prominently used form of ADR, and is generally far removed from modern mediation.

Significant changes in state policy concerning Australian industrial relations took place over the decade 1996 to 2007. The Howard government, with the introduction of the Workplace Relations Act 1996 (Cth), sought to shift the industrial system away from a collectivist approach, where unions and the AIRC had strong roles, to a more decentralised system of individual bargaining between employers and employees (Bamber *et al.*, 2000). The WRA Act 1996 (Cth) diminished the traditional role of the AIRC by placing the responsibility of resolving disputes at the enterprise level (Boulle, 2005). This allowed mediation to be used to resolve industrial relations disputes instead of the traditionally used conciliation.

The new 'Work Choices' Amendment came into effect in March 2006, and included a compulsory model dispute-resolution process that doesn't involve the AIRC. Mediation and other ADR processes have been encouraged by the government as a better option than the services provided by the AIRC. The government has realised the benefits of mediation to include the following (Van Gramberg, 2006):

- Mediation is cost saving;
- Avoids polarisation of parties;
- Is educative;
- Probes wider issues than the formal court system;
- Provides greater access to justice; and
- Gives disputants more control over the dispute process.

Workplace and Mediation

Mediation emerged on the industrial relations landscape in the late 1980s due to a number of economic and political factors which then induced managerial initiatives. According to Van Gramberg (2006), these changes have come from the implementation of human resource management policies and practices, which focuses on the individual worker, and rejects all other third parties such as unions, and the Australian Industrial relations Commission (AIRC). HRM together with the political and economic changes undertaken by the Howard government has created an environment where private ADR can be fostered in the workplace (Bamber *et al.*, 2000). The decline of unionism and the encouragement of individualisation in the workplace have encouraged the growth of private mediations. This is demonstrated in the industries with the lowest union rates such as in the private business sector having the greatest growth of mediation (Van Gramberg, 2006).

The Howard government's Work Choices Act, which came into effect on March 2006, made further legislative changes to deregulate the industrial relations system. A key element of the new changes was to weaken the powers of the AIRC in conciliation and arbitration by installing and encouraging private mediation in competition with the services provided by the AIRC.

Workplace conflicts can cover a great variety of disputes. For example disputes between staff members, allegations of harassment, contractual disputes relating to the terms and conditions of employment and workers-compensation claims (Boulle, 2005). At large, workplace disputes are between people who have an ongoing working relationship within a closed system, which indicate that mediation would be appropriate as a means of a dispute resolution process. However, in organisations there are many complex relationships, involving hierarchy, job security and competitiveness that make mediation a difficult task (Boulle, 2005).

Conflict Management

Society perceives conflict as something that gets in the way of progress, as a negative symptom of a relationship that one should cure as quickly as possible (Boulle, 2005). However, within the mediation profession conflict is seen as a fact of life and when properly managed it can have many benefits for the parties and constituents (Bagshaw 1999, Boulle, 2005). The benefits of conflict include the opportunity to renew relationships and make positive changes for the future. Mediation should be a productive process, where conflict can be managed and expressed safely (Bradford, 2006). It is the mediator's responsibility to let the parties express their emotions entailed in conflict safely. Allowing the parties to express these emotions may seem unhelpful in resolving the dispute, but if managed constructively these emotions may help towards a better relationship between the parties in the future.

Measuring the Effectiveness of Conflict Management

The ADR field has felt a need to define the effectiveness of dispute-resolution in a broad manner, including more than whether there was a settlement (Boulle, 2005). Mediation as a field of dispute resolution recognised there was more to measuring effectiveness, than a settlement. Mediation recognised in its own field that party satisfaction of the process and mediator competence could be measured. According to Boulle (2005) surveys of those who have participated in mediation reveal strong levels of satisfaction of the process.

Benefits of mediation may include:

- discovering parties' interests and priorities;
- healthy venting of emotions in a protected environment;
- an agreement to talk about a set agenda;
- identifying roles of the constituents, such as relatives and professional advisors; and
- knowledge of a constructive dispute resolution for use in a future dispute.

Confidentiality and Mediation

Confidentiality emerges as a powerful and attractive feature of mediation (Van Gramberg, 2006). The private and confidential aspect of mediation is in contrast with the courts and tribunals which are open to the public, and kept on record. Privacy is a big motivator for people to choose mediation over the courts or tribunals. Although mediation is promoted with confidentiality being one of the defining features of the process, it is not in reality as private and confidential as often claimed (Boulle, 2005). In some circumstances the parties agree that the mediation should not be private and confidential in parts or in whole.

Concerning the law there are limits to privacy and confidentiality, for example if their mediation entails abuse allegations, the mediator must disclose this information to the authorities. Also the more parties in a mediation the less likely it will be to maintain all the information as confidential. For example, some parties may be required to give an account of the mediation to outside constituents or authorities (Boulle, 2005).

Two competing principles affect the confidentiality of mediations. One principle involves upholding confidentiality as means to encourage people to settle out of the courts and avoid litigation, while the second principle states that all related facts in the mediation should be available to the courts.

A number of reasons exist for keeping mediation private and confidential; these include:

- it makes the mediation appealing;
- it provides a safe environment to disclose information and emotions;
- confidentiality makes mediation more effective by making parties talk realistically;
- confidentiality upholds mediators' reputations, as it reinforces impartiality; and
- confidentiality makes agreement more final, as there is little room to seek review.

Global Relevance

The rise of international trade law, continental trading blocs, the World Trade Organisation (and its opposing anti-globalisation movement), and use of the Internet, among other factors, seem to suggest that legal complexity has started to reach an intolerable and undesirable point. There may be no obvious way to determine which jurisdiction has precedence over which other, and there may be substantial resistance to settling a matter in any one place.

Accordingly, mediation may come into more widespread use, replacing formal legal and judicial processes sanctified by nation-states. Some people, like members of the anti-globalisation movement, believe such formal processes have quite thoroughly failed to provide real safety and closure guarantees that are pre-requisite to uniform rule of law.

Following an increasing awareness of the process, and a wider notion of its main aspects and eventual effects, some commentators in recent times have frequently proposed mediation for the resolution of international disputes, with attention to belligerent situations too.

However, as mediation ordinarily needs participation by the interested parties and it would be very difficult to impose it, in case one of the parts refuses this process it cannot be a solution.

The Fairness

As noted, mediation can only take place in an atmosphere where there is some agreement on safety, fairness and closure, usually provided by nation-states and their legal systems. But increasingly, disputes transcend international borders and include many parties who may be in unequal-power relationships.

In such circumstances, with many parties afraid to be identified or to make formal complaints, terminology or rules of standing or evidence slanted against some groups, and without power to enforce even "legally binding" contracts, some conclude that the process of mediation would not reasonably be said to be "fair".

Accordingly, even when a party offers to mediate and a mediator attempts to make the process fair, mediation itself might not operate as a fair process. In such cases, parties may pursue other means of dispute resolution.

From a more technical point of view, however, one must recall that the parties must require mediation, and very seldom can it be imposed by "non-parties" upon the parties. Therefore, in presence of entities that cannot be clearly identified, and that practically don't claim for their recognition as "parties", the professional experience of a mediator could only apply to a proposal of definition, that besides would always miss the constitutional elements of a mediation. Moreover, in such circumstances, the counter-party of these eventual entities would very likely deny any prestige of 'party' to the opponent, this not consenting any kind of treaty (in a correct mediation).

More generally, given that mediation ordinarily produces agreements containing elements to enforce the pacts with facts that can grant its effectiveness, note that other mechanisms apart from legal systems may ensure protection of the pacts: modern mediation frequently tends to define economic compensations and warranties too, generally considered quicker and more effective.

The concrete 'power' of an agreement is classically found in the *equilibre* of the pact, in the sincere conciliation of respective interests and in the inclusion of measures that would make the rupture of the pact very little convenient for the unfaithful party. Pacts that don't have such sufficient warranties are only academically effects of a mediation, but would never respect the deontology of the mediator.

13

Legal Perspective

Alternative Dispute Resolution

Alternative Dispute Resolution (ADR) (also known as External Dispute Resolution in some countries, such as Australia) includes dispute resolution processes and techniques that fall outside of the government judicial process. Despite historic resistance to ADR by both parties and their advocates, ADR has gained widespread acceptance among both the general public and the legal profession in recent years. In fact, some courts now require some parties to resort to ADR of some type, usually mediation, before permitting the parties' cases to be tried. The rising popularity of ADR can be explained by the increasing caseload of traditional courts, the perception that ADR imposes fewer costs than litigation, a preference for confidentiality, and the desire of some parties to have greater control over the selection of the individual or individuals who will decide their dispute.

Types

ADR is generally classified into at least four types: negotiation, mediation, collaborative law, and arbitration. (Sometimes a fifth type, conciliation, is included as well, but for present purposes it can be regarded as a form of mediation). ADR can used alongside existing legal systems such as Sharia Courts within Common Law jurisdictions such as the UK.

ADR traditions vary somewhat by country. There are significant common elements which justify a main topic, and each country or region's difference should be delegated to sub-pages.

ADR or Alternative Dispute Resolution is of two historic types. First, methods for resolving dispute outside of the official judicial mechanisms. Second, informal methods attached to or pendant to official judicial mechanisms. The methods are similar, whether or not they are pendant, and generally use similar tool or skill sets, which are basically subsets of the skills of negotatiation.

The basic ADR types are informal tribunals, informal mediative processes, formal tribunals and formal mediative processes. The classic formal tribunal forms of ADR are arbitration (both binding and advisory or non-binding) and private judges (either sitting alone, on panels or over summary jury trials). The classic formal mediative process is referall for mediation before a court appointed mediator or mediation panel. Structured transformative mediation as used by the US Postal Service is a formal process. Classic informal methods include social processes, referrals to non-formal authorities (such as a respected member of a trade or social group) and intercession. The major difference between formal and informal processes are: (a) pendancy to a court procedure, or (b) the possession or lack of a formal structure for the applicaiton of the procedure.

For example, freeform negotiation is merely the use of the tools without any process. Negotiation within a labour arbitration setting is the use of the tools within a highly formalised and controlled setting.

Referal to an ombudsman's office is a formal procedure. Informal referal to a co-worker known to help people work out issues is an informal procedure. HR departments are probably a formal procedure. Co-worker interventions are usually informal.

Conceptualising ADR in this way makes it easy to avoid confusing tools and methods (does negotiation once a law suit is filed cease to be ADR? If it is a tool, then the question is the wrong question) is medation ADR unless a court orders it? If you look at court orders and similar things as formalism, then the answer is clear, court annexed mediation is merely a formal ADR process.

In addition, dividing lines in ADR processes are often provider driven rather than consumer driven. For example, whether or not ADR professioanls should be paid or if being paid creates a conflict of interest that destroys the neutrality of the provider — that is a provider driven dividing line. The same is true as to whether ADR providers should be evaluative or not.

Generally, trade groups whose members are either paid or unpaid, competent to evaluate or not competent to evaluate, tend to drive these definitions; the same is true of transformative and other methodologies what claim to be the essential or only correct method. Educated consumers will often chose to use all of the methodologies depending on the needs and circumstances that they face and are the strongest force against trade group pressures.

Finally, it is important to realise that conflict resolution is the target of all the tools and processes. If a process leads to resolution, it is a dispute resolution process. If a tool or a skill helps with the process, then it is a tool in the dispute resolution spectrum. That is why such a wide variety of processes and tools fits within the topic of ADR, though ADR and Conflict Resolution can be divided by whether or not violent force is in play. ADR for when it is not, Conflict Resolution for when it is.

The salient features of each type are as follows:

1. In *negotiation*, participation is voluntary and there is no third party who facilitates the resolution process or imposes a resolution. (NB — a third party like a chaplain or organisational ombudsperson or social worker or a skilled friend may be coaching one or both of the parties behind the scene, a process called "Helping People Help Themselves").
2. In *mediation*, there is a third party, a mediator, who facilitates the resolution process (and may even suggest a resolution, typically known as a "mediator's proposal"), but does *not* impose a resolution on the parties. In some countries (for example, the United Kingdom), ADR is synonymous with what is generally referred to as mediation in other countries.
3. In *collaborative law* or *collaborative divorce*, each party has an attorney who facilitates the resolution process within

specifically contracted terms. The parties reach agreement with support of the attorneys (who are trained in the process) and mutually-agreed experts. No one imposes a resolution on the parties. However, the process is a formalised process that is part of the litigation and court system. Rather than being an Alternative Resolution methodology it is a litigation varient that happens to rely on ADR like attitudes and processes.

4. In *arbitration*, participation is typically voluntary, and there is a third party who, as a private judge, imposes a resolution. Arbitrations often occur because parties to contracts agree that any future dispute concerning the agreement will be resolved by arbitration. This is known as a 'Scott Avery Clause'. In recent years, the enforceability of arbitration clauses, particularly in the context of consumer agreements (e.g., credit card agreements), has drawn scrutiny from courts. Although parties may appeal arbitration outcomes to courts, such appeals face an exacting standard of review.

Beyond the basic types of alternative dispute resolutions there are other different forms of ADR:

- *Case Evaluation:* A non-binding process in which parties present the facts and the issues to a neutral case evaluator who advises the parties on the strengths and weaknesses of their respective positions, and assesses how the dispute is likely to be decided by a jury or other adjudicator.
- *Early Neutral Evaluation:* A process that takes place soon after a case has been filed in court. The case is referred to an expert who is asked to provide a balanced and neutral evaluation of the dispute. The evaluation of the expert can assist the parties in assessing their case and may influence them towards a settlement.
- *Family Group Conference:* A meeting between members of a family and members of their extended related group. At this meeting (or often a series of meetings) the family becomes involved in learning skills for interaction and in making a plan to stop the abuse or other ill-treatment between its members.

- *Neutral Fact-finding:* A process where a neutral third party, selected either by the disputing parties or by the court, investigates an issue and reports or testifies in court. The neutral fact-finding process is particularly useful for resolving complex scientific and factual disputes.
- *Ombuds:* Third party selected by an institution – for example a university, hospital, corporation or government agency – to investigate complaints by employees, clients or constituents. The ombuds works within the institution to look into complaints independently and impartially.

"Alternative" dispute resolution is usually considered to be alternative to litigation. It also can be used as a colloquialism for allowing a dispute to drop or as an alternative to violence.

In recent years there has been more discussion about taking a systems approach in order to offer different kinds of options to people who are in conflict, and to foster "appropriate" dispute resolution. That is, some cases and some complaints in fact ought to go to formal grievance or to court or to the police or to a compliance officer or to a government IG. Other conflicts could be settled by the parties if they had enough support and coaching, and yet other cases need mediation or arbitration. Thus, "alternative" dispute resolution simply means a method that is not the courts. "Appropriate" dispute resolution considers all the possible responsible options for conflict resolution that are relevant for a given issue.

Arbitration and Mediation are the best known and most commonly used forms of ADR within the UK. However, in recent years Adjudication is rapidly gaining notoriety as a quick, fair and cheap was to settle disputes.

ADR can increasingly be conducted online, which is known as online dispute resolution (ODR, which is mostly a buzzword and an attempt to create a distinctive product). It should be noted, however, that ODR services can be provided by government entities, and as such may form part of the litigation process. Moreover, they can be provided on a global scale, where no effective domestic remedies are available to disputing parties, as in the case of the UDRP and domain name disputes. In this respect, ODR might not satisfy the "alternative" element of ADR.

Country Specific Examples

China

Chinese trained mediators have a long history and were practicing in court annexed mediations in the United States more than thirty years ago.

Modern Era

Traditional peoples' mediation has always involved the parties remaining in contact for most or all of the mediation session. The innovation of separating the parties after (or sometimes before) a joint session and conducting the rest of the process without the parties in the same area was a major innovation and one that dramatically improved mediation's success rate.

Traditional arbitration involved heads of trade guilds or other dominant authorities settling disputes. The modern innovation was to have commercial vendors of arbitrators, often ones with little or no social or political dominance over the parties. The advantage was that such persons are much more readily available. The disadvantage is that it does not involve the community of the parties. When wool contract arbitration was conducted by senior guild officials, the arbitrator combined a seasoned expert on the subject matter with a socially dominant individual whose patronage, good will and opinion were important.

Private judges and summary jury trials are cost and time savings processes that have had limited penetration due to the alternatives becoming more robust and accepted.

Iceland

The Saga of Burnt Njal is the story of a mediator who was so successful that he eventually threatened the local power structure. It ends in tragedy with the unlawful burning of Njal alive in his home, the escape of a friend of the family, a mini-war and the eventual ending of the dispute by the intermarriage of the two strongest survivors. It illustrates that mediation was a powerful process in Iceland before the era of kings.

Roman Empire

Latin has a number of terms for mediator that predate the Roman Empire. Any time there are formal adjudicative processes it appears that there are informal ones as well. It is probably fruitless to attempt to determine which group had mediation first.

India

Alternative dispute resolution in India is not new and it was in existence even under the previous Arbitration Act, 1940. The Arbitration and Conciliation Act, 1996 has been enacted to accommodate the harmonisation mandates of UNCITRAL Model. To streamline the Indian legal system the traditional civil law known as Code of Civil Procedure, (CPC) 1908 has also been amended and section 89 has been introduced. Section 89 (1) of CPC provides an option for the settlement of disputes outside the court. It provides that where it appears to the court that there exist elements, which may be acceptable to the parties, the court may formulate the terms of a possible settlement and refer the same for arbitration, conciliation, mediation or judicial settlement.

Due to extremely slow judicial process, there has been a big thrust on Alternate Dispute Resolution mechanisms in India. While Arbitration and Conciliation Act, 1996 is a fairly standard western approach towards ADR, the Lok Adalat system constituted under National Legal Services Authority Act, 1987 is a uniquely Indian approach.

Arbitration and Conciliation Act

Part I of this act formalises the process of Arbitration and Part III formalises the process of Conciliation. (Part II is about Enforcement of Foreign Awards under New York and Geneva Conventions.)

Arbitration

The process of arbitration can start only if there exists a valid Arbitration Agreement between the parties prior to the emergence of the dispute. As per Section 7, such an agreement must be in writing. The contract regarding which the dispute exists, must either contain an arbitration clause or must refer to a separate document signed by the parties containing the arbitration agreement. The existence of an arbitration agreement can also be inferred by written correspondence such as letters, talex, or telegrams which provide a record of the agreement. An exchange of statement of claim and defence in which existence of an arbitration agreement is alleged by one party and not denied by other is also considered as valid written arbitration agreement.

Any party to the dispute can start the process of appointing arbitrator and if the other party does not cooperate, the party can approach the office of Chief Justice for appointement of an arbitrator. There are only two grounds upon which a party can challenge the appointment of an arbitrator — reasonable doubt in the immpartiality of the arbitrator and the lack of proper qualification of the arbitrator as required by the arbitration agreement. A sole arbitrator or a panel of arbitrators so appointed constitute the Arbitration Tribunal.

Except for some interim measures, there is very little scope for judicial intervention in the arbitration process. The arbitration tribunal has jurisdiction over its own jurisdiction. Thus, if a party wants to challenge the jurisdiction of the arbitration tribunal, it can do so only before the tribunal itself. If the tribunal rejects the request, there is little the party can do accept to approach a court after the tribunal makes an award. Section 34 provides certain grounds upon which a party can appeal to the principal civil court of original jurisdiction for setting aside the award.

Once the period for filing an appeal for setting aside an award is over, or if such an appeal is rejected, the award is binding on the parties and is considered as a decree of the court.

Conciliation

Conciliation is a less formal form of arbitration. This process does not require an existence of any prior agreement. Any party can request the other party to appoint a conciliator. One conciliator is preferred but two or three are also allowed. In case of multiple conciliators, all must act jointly. If a party rejects an offer to conciliate, there can be no conciliation.

Parties may submit statements to the conciliator describing the general nature of the dispute and the points at issue. Each party sends a copy of the statement to the other. The conciliator may request further details, may ask to meet the parties, or communicate with the parties orally or in writing. Parties may even submit suggestions for the settlement of the dispute to the conciliator.

When it appears to the conciliator that elements of settlement exist, he may draw up the terms of settlement and send it to the parties for their acceptance. If both the parties sign the settlement document, it shall be final and binding on both.

Note that in USA, this process is similar to Mediation. However, in India, Mediation is different from Conciliation and is a completely informal type of ADR mechanism.

Lok Adalat

It roughly means, "Peoples' court". India has had a long history of resolving disputes through the mediation of village elders. The system of Lok Adalats is an improvement on that and is based on Gandhian principles. This is a non-adversarial system, where by mock courts (called *Lok Adalats*) are held by the State Authority, District Authority, Supreme Court Legal Services Committee, High Court Legal Services Committee, or Taluk Legal Services Committee, periodically for exercising such jurisdiction as they thinks fit. These are usually presided by retired judge, social activists, or members of legal profession. It does not have jurisdiction on matters related to non-compoundable offences.

There is no court fee and no rigid procedural requirement (i.e. no need to follow process given by Civil Procedure Code or Evidence Act), which makes the process very fast. Parties can directly interact with the judge, which is not possible in regular courts.

Cases that are pending in regular courts can be transferred to a Lok Adalat if both the parties agree. A case can also be transferred to a Lok Adalat if one party applies to the court and the court sees some chance of settlement after giving an opportunity of being heard to the other party.

The focus in Lok Adalats is on compromise. When no compromise is reached, the matter goes back to the court. However, if a compromise is reached, an award is made and is binding on the parties. It is enforced as a decree of a civil court. An important aspect is that the award is final and cannot be appealed, not even under Article 226 because it is a judgement by consent.

All proceeding of a Lok Adalat are deemed to be Judicial proceedings and every Lok Adalat is deemed to be a Civil Court.

Permanent Lok Adalat for Public Utility Services: In order to get over the major drawback in the existing scheme of organisation of Lok Adalats under Chapter VI of the Legal Services Authorities Act, 1987, in which if the parties do not arrive at any compromise or settlement, the unsettled case is either returned back to the Court of law or the parties are advised to seek remedy in a court of law, which causes unnecessary delay in dispensation of justice, Chapter VI A was introduced in the Legal Services Authorities Act, 1987, by Act No. 37/2002 with effect from 11-06-2002 providing for a Permanent Lok Adalat to deal with pre-litigation, conciliation and settlement of disputes relating to Public Utility Services, as defined u/sec.22 A of the Legal Services Authorities Act, 1987, at pre-litigation stage itself, which would result in reducing the work load of the regular courts to a great extent.

- Permanent Lok Adalat for Public Utility Services, Hyderabad, India.

Lok Adalat (people's courts), established by the government to settle dispute through conciliation and compromise. The First Lok Adalat was held in Chennai in 1986. Lok Adalat accepts the cases which could be settled by conciliation and compromise, and pending in the regular courts within their jurisdiction.

The Lok Adalat is presided over by a sitting or retired judicial officer as the chairman, with two other members, usually a lawyer and a social worker. There is no court fee. If the case is already filed in the regular court, the fee paid will be refunded if the dispute is settled at the Lok Adalat. The procedural laws, and the Evidence Act are not strictly followed while assessing the merits of the claim by the Lok Adalat.

Main condition of the Lok Adalat is that both parties in dispute should agree for settlement. The decision of the Lok Adalat is binding on the parties to the dispute and its order is capable of execution through legal process. No appeal lies against the order of the Lok Adalat.

Lok Adalat is very effective in settlement of money claims. Disputes like partition suits, damages and matrimonial cases can also be easily settled before Lok Adalat as the scope for compromise through an approach of give and take is high in these cases.

Lok Adalat is a boon to the litigant public, where they can get their disputes settled fast and free of cost.

Fordham Law School's Dispute Resolution Programme

Fordham Law School's Dispute Resolution programme placed in the top 10 of US News and World Report's 2008 rankings of the best Dispute Resolution programmes in the nation, according to the recently-released rankings. Along with Fordham's Clinical Training programme, the Dispute Resolution programme is the top-ranked speciality programme at Fordham Law School. The Alternative Dispute Resolution programme at Fordham combines an integrated agenda of teaching, scholarship, and practice in conflict resolution within the national and international communities. In addition to the classroom and clinical experience, the law school's student-run Dispute Resolution Society competes in ABA-sponsored interschool competitions as well as international mediation and arbitration competitions. In 2008, the Society's teams won the ABA Regional Negotiation Competition, placed third overall in the International Chamber of Commerce Commercial Mediation Competition in Paris, and reached the semi-finals of the Willem C. Vis (East) International Commercial Arbitration Competition in Hong Kong. Additionally, Fordham's Dispute Resolution Society hosts an annual symposium on current Dispute Resolution topics and also teaches a class on dispute resolution skills to seniors at the Martin Luther King, Jr. High School in New York City.

Cornell University's Scheinman Institute on Conflict Resolution

Cornell's ILR School has joined forces with Cornell's Law School to present the country's most comprehensive conflict resolution programme focusing on workplace alternative dispute resolution (ADR). The Martin and Laurie Scheinman Institute on Conflict Resolution mission is to educate the next generation of neutrals — arbitrators, mediators and facilitators — who can help resolve disputes between employers and employees, both unionised and non-unionised. The Institute provides training for undergraduate and graduate students, consultation and evaluation, and conducts research. It also offers courses in two-to-five day sessions designed for professionals who are interested in or practicing in the workplace dispute resolution field. These highly intensive and participatory courses are coordinated by Cornell ILR faculty and are held in the ILR School's conference centre in Manhattan and on the Ithaca campus. Participants can earn two certificates, Workplace Alternative Dispute Resolution and Conflict Management and Labour Arbitration.

Straus Institute For Dispute Resolution

Pepperdine University School of Law's Straus Institute for Dispute Resolution provides professional training and academic programmes in dispute resolution including a Certificate, Masters in Dispute Resolution (MDR) and Masters of Law in Dispute Resolution (LLM). Straus provides education to law and graduate students, as well as mid-career professionals in areas of mediation, negotiation, arbitration, international dispute resolution and peacemaking. The Straus Institute has consistently ranked the number one Dispute Resolution school in the nation for the past 3 years, and has remained among the top 10 schools over the last decade.

CUNY Dispute Resolution Consortium

The City University of New York Dispute Resolution Consortium (CUNY DRC) serves as an intellectual home to dispute-resolution faculty, staff and students at the City University of New York and to the diverse dispute-resolution community in New York City. At the United States' largest urban university system, the CUNY DRC has become a focal point for furthering academic and applied conflict resolution work in one of the world's most diverse cities. The CUNY DRC conducts research and innovative programme development, has co-organised countless conferences, sponsored training programmes, resolved a wide range of intractable conflicts, published research working papers and a newsletter. It also maintains an extensive database of those interested in dispute resolution in New York City, a website with resources for dispute resolvers in New York City and since 9/11, the CUNY DRC assumed a leadership role for dispute-resolvers in New York City by establishing an extensive electronic mailing list, sponsoring monthly breakfast meetings, conducting research on responses to catastrophes, and managing a public awareness initiative to further the work of dispute resolvers.

CPR Institute for Dispute Resolution

- The International Institute for Conflict Prevention and Resolution, known as the CPR Institute, is a New York City membership-based non-profit organisation that promotes excellence and innovation in public and private dispute resolution, serving as a primary multinational resource for avoidance, management, and resolution of business-related disputes.

The CPR Institute was founded in 1979 as the Centre for Public Resources by a coalition of leading corporate general counsel dedicated to identifying and applying appropriate alternative solutions to business disputes, thereby mitigating the extraordinary costs of lengthy court trials.

CPR's mission is "to spearhead innovation and promote excellence in public and private dispute resolution, and to serve as a primary multinational resource for avoidance, management and resolution of business-related and other disputes." CPR is a non-profit educational corporation existing under the New York state laws, and is tax exempt pursuant to Section 501(c)(3) of the US Internal Revenue Code.

It is governed by a board of directors, and its priorities and policies are guided in large part by consultation with an executive advisory committee. Its funding derives in principal part from the annual contributions of its member organisations, and from its mission-related programming. The various operations and activities that fulfil the Institute's mission are captured in the acronym of its name:

C: CPR convenes legal and business leadership to develop, and encourage the exchange of, best practices in avoiding, managing and resolving disputes.

P: CPR publishes its own work and that of other like-minded organisations, making resources available to a global community of problem-solvers.

R: CPR helps to resolve complex disputes among sophisticated parties, by devising rules, protocols and best practices, and by providing disputants with resources and consulting expertise in selecting appropriate methods and neutrals to assist in the dispute resolution process.

ICAR

Established at George Mason as an alternative to a sociology programme due to Virgina's then policy against duplicating graduate schools, it was the nations first major dispute resolution graduate programme. It has been a major success.

Arbitration

Arbitration, a form of Alternative Dispute Resolution (ADR), is a legal technique for the resolution of disputes outside the courts, wherein the parties to a dispute refer it to one or more persons (the "arbitrators", "arbiters" or "arbitral tribunal"), by whose decision (the "award") they agree to be bound. It is a settlement technique in which a third party reviews the case and imposes a decision that is legally binding for both sides. Other forms of ADR include mediation (a form of settlement negotiation facilitated by a neutral third party) and non-binding resolution by experts. It is more helpful, however, simply to classify arbitration as a form of binding dispute resolution, equivalent to litigation in the courts, and entirely distinct from the other forms of dispute resolution, such as negotiation, mediation, or determinations by experts, which are usually non-binding. Arbitration is most commonly used for the resolution of commercial disputes, particularly in the context of international commercial transactions. The use of arbitration is far more controversial in consumer and employment matters, where arbitration is not voluntary but is instead imposed on consumers or employees through fine-print contracts, denying individuals of their right to access the courts.

Arbitration can be either voluntary or mandatory and can be either binding or non-binding. Non-binding arbitration is, on the surface, similar to mediation. However, the principal distinction is that whereas a mediator will try to help the parties find a middle ground to compromise at, the arbitrator remains totally removed from the settlement process and will only give a determination of liability and, if appropriate, an indication of the quantum of damages payable.

History

It is not known exactly when formal non-judicial arbitration first began but it can be said with some certainty that arbitration, as a way of resolving disputes predates formal courts. Records from ancient Egypt attest to its use especially with high priests and their interaction with the public. Arbitration was popular both in ancient Greece and in Rome.

Under English law, the first law on arbitration was the Arbitration Act 1697, but when it was passed arbitration was already common. The first recorded judicial decision relating to arbitration was in England in 1610. The noted Elizabethan English legal scholar Sir Edward Coke refers to an earlier decision dating from the reign of Edward IV (which ended in 1483). Early arbitrations at common law suffered from the fatal weakness that either party to the dispute could withdraw the arbitrator's mandate right up until the delivery of the award if things appeared to be going against them (this was rectified in the 1697 Act).

The Jay Treaty of 1794 between Britain and the United States sent unresolved issues regarding debts and boundaries to arbitration, which took 7 years and proved successful.

In the first part of the 20th century, many countries (France and the United States being good examples) began to pass laws sanctioning and even promoting the use of private adjudication as an alternative to what was perceived to be inefficient court systems.

The growth of international trade, however, brought greater sophistication to a process that had previously been largely *ad hoc* in relation to disputes between merchants resolved under the auspices of the *lex mercatoria*. As trade grew, so did the practice of arbitration, eventually leading to the creation of a variant now known as international arbitration, as a means for resolving disputes under international commercial contracts.

Today, arbitration also occurs online, in what is commonly referred to as Online Dispute Resolution, or ODR. Typically, ODR proceedings occur following the filing of a claim online, with the proceedings taking place over the internet, and judgement rendered on the basis of documentation presented.

Nature

Arbitration is a proceeding in which a dispute is resolved by an impartial adjudicator whose decision the parties to the dispute have agreed will be final and binding. Arbitration is not the same as:

- judicial proceedings, although in some jurisdictions, court proceedings are sometimes referred as arbitrations;
- Alternative Dispute Resolution (or ADR);
- expert determination; and
- mediation.

Advantages and Disadvantages: Parties often seek to resolve their disputes through arbitration because of a number of perceived potential advantages over judicial proceedings:

- when the subject matter of the dispute is highly technical, arbitrators with an appropriate degree of expertise can be appointed;
- arbitration is often faster than litigation in court;
- arbitration can be cheaper and more flexible for businesses;
- arbitral proceedings and an arbitral award are generally non-public, and can be made confidential;
- because of the provisions of the New York Convention 1958, arbitration awards are generally easier to enforce in other nations than court judgements; and
- in most legal systems, there are very limited avenues for appeal of an arbitral award.

However, some of the disadvantages of arbitration can be that:

- arbitration agreements are sometimes contained in ancillary agreements, or in small print in other agreements, and consumers and employees sometimes do not know in advance that they have agreed to mandatory binding pre-dispute arbitration by purchasing a product or taking a job;
- if the arbitration is mandatory and binding, the parties waive their rights to access the courts and have a judge or jury decide the case;
- in some arbitration agreements, the parties are required to pay for the arbitrators, which adds an additional layer of legal cost that can be prohibitive, especially in small consumer disputes;

- in some arbitration agreements and systems, the recovery of attorneys' fees is unavailable, making it difficult or impossible for consumers or employees to get legal representation; however most arbitration codes and agreements provide for the same relief that could be granted in court;
- if the arbitrator or the arbitration forum depends on the corporation for repeat business, there may be an inherent incentive to rule against the consumer or employee;
- there are very limited avenues for appeal, which means that an erroneous decision cannot be easily overturned;
- although usually thought to be speedier, when there are multiple arbitrators on the panel, juggling their schedules for hearing dates in long cases can lead to delays;
- in some legal systems, arbitral awards have fewer enforcement remedies than judgements; although in the United States, arbitration awards are enforced in the same manner as court judgements and have the same effect;
- arbitrators are generally unable to enforce interlocutory measures against a party, making it easier for a party to take steps to avoid enforcement of an award, such as the relocation of assets offshore;
- rule of applicable law is not necessarily binding on the arbitrators, although they cannot disregard the law.
- discovery may be more limited in arbitration; and
- the potential to generate billings by attorneys may be less than pursuing the dispute through trial.

Arbitrability

By their nature, the subject matter of some disputes are not capable of arbitration. In general, two groups of legal procedures cannot be subjected to arbitration:

- Procedures which necessarily lead to a determination which the parties to the dispute may not enter into an agreement upon: Some court procedures lead to judgements which bind all members of the general public, or public authorities in their capacity as such, or third parties, or which are being conducted in the public interest. *Examples*: Until relatively recently (1980s), anti-trust matters were not arbitrable in the United States. Matters relating to crimes, status and family law are generally not considered to be arbitrable, as the power of the parties to enter into an agreement upon these matters is at least restricted. However, most other disputes that involve private rights between two parties can be resolved using arbitration. In some disputes, parts of claims may be arbitrable and other parts not.

For example, in a dispute over patent infringement, a determination of whether a patent has been infringed could be adjudicated upon by an arbitration tribunal, but the validity of a patent could not: As patents are subject to a system of public registration, an arbitral panel would have no power to order the relevant body to rectify any patent registration based upon its determination.

- Some legal orders exclude or restrict the possibility of arbitration for reasons of the protection of weaker members of the public, e.g. consumers. *Examples*: German law excludes disputes over the rental of living space from any form of arbitration while arbitration agreements with consumers are only considered valid if they are signed by either party, and if the signed document does not bear any other content than the arbitration agreement.

Arbitration Agreement

In theory, arbitration is a consensual process; a party cannot be forced to arbitrate a dispute unless he agrees to do so. In practice, however, many fine-print arbitration agreements are inserted in situations in which consumers and employees have no bargaining power. Moreover, arbitration clauses are frequently placed within sealed users' manuals within products, within lengthy click-through agreements on websites, and in other contexts in which meaningful consent is not realistic. Such agreements are generally divided into two types:

- Agreements which provide that, if a dispute should arise, it will be resolved by arbitration. These will generally be normal contracts, but they contain an arbitration clause.
- Agreements which are signed after a dispute has arisen, agreeing that the dispute should be resolved by arbitration (sometimes called a "submission agreement").

The former is the far more prevalent type of arbitration agreement. Sometimes, legal significance attaches to the type of arbitration agreement. For example, in certain Commonwealth countries, it is possible to provide that each party should bear their own costs in a conventional arbitration clause, but not in a submission agreement.

In keeping with the informality of the arbitration process, the law is generally keen to uphold the validity of arbitration clauses even when they lack the normal formal language associated with legal contracts. Clauses which have been upheld include:

- "arbitration in London — English law to apply";
- "suitable arbitration clause";
- "arbitration, if any, by ICC Rules in London".

The courts have also upheld clauses which specify resolution of disputes other than in accordance with a specific legal system. These include provision indicating:

- that the arbitrators "must not necessarily judge according to the strict law but as a general rule ought chiefly to consider the principles of practical business";
- "internationally accepted principles of law governing contractual relations".

Agreements to refer disputes to arbitration generally have a special status in the eyes of the law. For example, in disputes on a contract, a common defence is to plead the contract is void and thus any claim based upon it fails. It follows that if a party successfully claims that a contract is void, then each clause contained within the contract, including the arbitration clause, would be void. However, in most countries, the courts have accepted that:

1. A contract can only be declared void by a court or other tribunal; and
2. If the contract (valid or otherwise) contains an arbitration clause, then the proper forum to determine whether the contract is void or not, is the arbitration tribunal.

Arguably, either position is potentially unfair; if a person is made to sign a contract under duress, and the contract contains an arbitration clause highly favourable to the other party, the dispute may still referred to that arbitration tribunal. Conversely a court may be persuaded that the arbitration agreement itself is void having been signed under duress.

However, most courts will be reluctant to interfere with the general rule which does allow for commercial expediency; any other solution (where one first had to go to court to decide whether one had to go to arbitration) would be self defeating.

Applicable Laws

Arbitration is subject to different laws. These may be summarised as follows:

- The law governing the arbitration agreement;
- The law governing the arbitral tribunal and its proceedings (lex arbitri - procedural law);
- The law governing the substance of the dispute;
- The law governing recognition and enforcement of the award.

Severability and Law Governing the Arbitration Agreement

The arbitration agreement which is part of the main contract (often referred to as "container contract") is governed by the law which governs the main contract. An important feature of arbitration, however, is severability — the fact that arbitration agreement lives a life of its own and is autonomous of the main agreement. Invoking the invalidity of the main agreement may not necessarily bring with it the invalidity of the arbitration clause. Another feature closely tied to this is "competence-competence" — the ability of the arbitration tribunal to decide on its own jurisdiction. Therefore, a party who is trying to avoid arbitration at an early stage by claiming that the main contract is invalid will face the arbitration agreement separate from the main one and the arbitrators deciding on their own competence.

In American law, this was recognised by the *Prima Paint Corp. v. Flood & Conklin Mfg. Co.* decision of the US Supreme Court.

Seat of the Arbitration

Most legal systems recognise the concept of a "seat" of the arbitration, which is a geographical and legal jurisdiction to which the arbitration is tied. The seat will normally determine the procedural rules (*lex arbitri*) which the arbitration follows, and the courts which exercise jurisdiction over the seat will have a supervisory role over the conduct of the arbitration.

Parties to the arbitration are free to choose the seat of arbitration and often do so in practice. If they do not, the arbitral tribunal will do it for them. Whereas it is possible to detach procedural law from the seat of arbitration (e.g. seat in Switzerland, English procedural law) this creates confusion as it subjects the arbitration to two controlling and possibly conflicting laws. The procedural law of arbitration, normally determined by the seat, ought to be distinguished from the procedure that the arbitration panel will follow. The latter refers to daily operation of the arbitration and is normally determined either by the institution in question (if arbitration is institutional, e.g. ICC Rules) or by reference to a ready-made procedure (such as the UNCITRAL Rules).

The seat of arbitration might not be the same as the place where proceedings are actually happening. Thus, for instance, an ICC arbitration may have its seat in London (and therefore be governed by the English *lex arbitri* and ICC procedural rules) and most sessions may take place outside the UK.

Law Applicable to Procedure

The essential matters of procedure — such as any disagreement over the appointment or replacement of arbitrators, the jurisdiction of the tribunal itself, or the validity of an arbitration award — are determined by the procedural law of the seat of the arbitration, and may be decided by recourse to courts. The parties normally influence this through their choice of the seat of arbitration or directly through choice of procedural law.

All other matters of procedure are generally determined by the arbitral tribunal itself (depending on national law and respect for due process) and the preferences of the arbitrators, the parties, and their counsel. The arbitrators' power to determine procedural matters normally includes:

- mode of submitting (and challenging) evidence;
- time and place of any hearings;
- language and translations;
- disclosure of documents and other evidence;

- use of pleadings and/or interrogatories;
- the appointment of experts and assessors.

Law Applicable to Substance

Parties in a commercial dispute will often choose the law applicable to the substance of their dispute. In fact, they are more likely to choose substantive than procedural law as this will have direct impact on the outcome of their dispute. This choice is usually expressed in the arbitration clause itself or at least in part of the contract where the clause is located.

If the parties do not choose the applicable law the arbitral tribunal will. This is normally interpreted as the ability of the tribunal to choose the choice-of-law rules which will, in turn, point to the applicable law. The arbitrators are not strictly speaking bound by public policy order or mandatory rules of third states but will normally observe them as that increases the chance of the award being recognised.

The tribunal may decide *ex aequo et bono* only if the parties have expressly authorised them to do so.

Law Applicable to Recognition and Enforcement

The law that applies to issues of recognition will always be the law of the state where this recognition is sought. In a large number of states this will be governed by 1958 New York Convention which harmonises the recognition and enforcement of foreign arbitral awards.

Sources of Law

States regulate arbitration through a variety of laws. The main body of law applicable to arbitration is normally contained either in the national Private International Law Act (as is the case in Switzerland) or in a separate law on arbitration (as is the case in England). In addition to this, a number of national procedural laws may also contain provisions relating to arbitration.

By far the most important international instrument on arbitration law is the 1958 New York Convention on Recognition and Enforcement of Foreign Arbitral Awards. Some other relevant international instruments are:

- The Geneva Protocol of 1923;
- The Geneva Convention of 1927;
- The European Convention of 1961;
- The Washington Convention of 1965 (governing settlement of international investment disputes);
- The UNCITRAL Model Law (providing a model for a national law of arbitration);
- The UNCITRAL Arbitration Rules (providing a set of rules for an *ad hoc* arbitration).

Arbitral Tribunal

The term *arbitral tribunal* is used to denote the arbitrator or arbitrators sitting to determine the dispute. The composition of the arbitral tribunal can vary enormously, with either a sole arbitrator sitting, two or more arbitrators, with or without a chairman or umpire, and various other combinations.

In most jurisdictions, an arbitrator enjoys immunity from liability for anything done or omitted whilst acting as arbitrator unless the arbitrator acts in bad faith.

Arbitrations are usually divided into two types:

- *ad hoc* arbitrations and *administered* arbitrations.

In *ad hoc* arbitrations, the arbitral tribunals are appointed by the parties or by an appointing authority chosen by the parties. After the tribunal has been formed, the appointing authority will normally have no other role and the arbitation will be managed by the tribunal.

In *administered* arbitration, the arbitration will be administered by a professional arbitration institution providing arbitration services, such as the LCIA in London or the ICC in Paris. Normally the arbitration institution also will be the appointing authority.

Arbitration institutions tend to have their own rules and procedures, and may be more formal. They also tend to be more expensive, and, for procedural reasons, slower.

Duties of the Tribunal

The duties of a tribunal will be determined by a combination of the provisions of the arbitration agreement and by the procedural laws which apply in the seat of the arbitration. The extent to which the laws of the seat of the arbitration permit "party autonomy" (the ability of the parties to set out their own procedures and regulations) determines the interplay between the two.

However, in almost all countries the tribunal owes several non-derogable duties. These will normally be:

- to act fairly and impartially between the parties, and to allow each party a reasonable opportunity to put their case and to deal with the case of their opponent (sometimes shortened to: complying with the rules of "natural justice"); and
- to adopt procedures suitable to the circumstances of the particular case, so as to provide a fair means for resolution of the dispute.

Arbitral Awards

Although arbitration awards are characteristically an award of damages against a party, in many jurisdictions tribunals have a range of remedies that can form a part of the award. These may include:

1. payment of a sum of money (conventional damages);
2. the making of a "declaration" as to any matter to be determined in the proceedings;
3. in some jurisdictions, the tribunal may have the same power as a court to:
   a. order a party to do or refrain from doing something (injunctive relief);
   b. to order specific performance of a contract;
   c. to order the rectification, setting aside or cancellation of a deed or other document.
4. In other jurisdictions, however, unless the parties have expressly granted the arbitrators the right to decide such matters, the tribunal's powers may be limited to deciding whether a party is entitled to damages. It may not have the legal authority to order injunctive relief, issue a declaration, or rectify a contract, such powers being reserved to the exclusive jurisdiction of the courts.

Enforcement of Arbitration Awards

One of the reasons that arbitration is so popular in international trade as a means of dispute resolution, is that it is often easier to enforce an arbitration award in a foreign country than it is to enforce a judgement of the court.

Under the New York Convention 1958, an award issued a contracting state can generally be freely enforced in any other contracting state, only subject to certain, limited defences.

Only foreign arbitration awards can be subject to recognition and enforcement pursuant to the New York Convention. An arbitral decision is foreign where the award was made in a state other than the state of recognition or where foreign procedural law was used.

Virtually every significant commercial country in the world is a party to the Convention, but relatively few countries have a comprehensive network for cross-border enforcement of judgements of the court.

The other characteristic of cross-border enforcement of arbitration awards that makes them appealing to commercial parties is that they are not limited to awards of damages. Whereas in most countries only monetary judgements are enforceable in the cross-border context, no such restrictions are imposed on arbitration awards and so it is theoretically possible (although unusual in practice) to obtain an injunction or an order for specific performance in an arbitration proceeding which could then be enforced in another New York Convention contracting state.

The New York Convention is not actually the only treaty dealing with cross-border enforcement of arbitration awards. The earlier Geneva Convention on the Execution of Foreign Arbitral Awards 1927 remains in force, but the success of the New York Convention means that the Geneva Convention is rarely utilised in practise.

Arbitration with Sovereign Governments: Certain international conventions exist in relation to the enforcement of awards against states.

- The Washington Convention 1965 relates to settlement of investment disputes between states and citizens of other countries. The Convention created the International Centre for Settlement of Investment Disputes (or ICSID). Compared to other arbitration institutions, relatively few awards have been rendered under ICSID.

- The Algiers Declaration of 1981 established the Iran-US Claims Tribunal to adjudicate claims of American corporations and individuals in relation to expropriated property during the Islamic revolution in Iran in 1979. The tribunal has not been a notable success, and has even been held by an English court to be void under its own governing law.

Challenge

Generally speaking, by their nature, arbitration proceedings tend not to be subject to appeal, in the ordinary sense of the word.

However, in most countries, the court maintains a supervisory role to set aside awards in extreme cases, such as fraud or in the case of some serious legal irregularity on the part of the tribunal.

Only domestic arbitral awards (i.e. those where the seat of arbitration is located in the same state as the court seised) are subject to set aside procedure.

In American arbitration law there exists a small but significant body of case law which deals with the power of the courts to intervene where the decision of an arbitrator is in fundamental disaccord with the applicable principles of law or the contract.

Unfortunately there is little agreement amongst the different American judgements and textbooks as to whether such a separate doctrine exists at all, or the circumstances in which it would apply. There does not appear to be any recorded judicial decision in which it has been applied. However, conceptually, to the extent it exists, the doctrine would be an important derogation from the general principle that awards are not subject to review by the courts.

Costs

In many legal systems — both common law and civil law — it is normal practice for the courts to award legal costs against a losing party, with the winner becoming entitled to recover an approximation of what it spent in pursuing its claim (or in defence of a claim). The United States is a notable exception to this rule, as except for certain extreme cases, a prevailing party in a US legal proceeding does not become entitled to recoup its legal fees from the losing party.

Like the courts, arbitral tribunals generally have the same power to award costs in relation to the determination of the dispute. In international arbitration as well as domestic arbitrations conducted in countries where courts may award costs against a losing party, the arbitral tribunal will also determine the portion of the arbitrators' fees that the losing party is required to bear.

Nomenclatures

As methods of dispute resolution, arbitration procedure can be varied to suit the needs of the parties. Certain specific "types" of arbitration procedure have developed, particularly in North America.

- Judicial Arbitration is, usually, not arbitration at all, but merely a court process which refers to itself as arbitration, such as small claims arbitration before the County Courts in the United Kingdom.
- High-Low Arbitration, or Bracketed Arbitration, is an arbitration wherein the parties to the dispute agree in advance the limits within which the arbitral tribunal must render its award. It is only generally useful where liability is not in dispute, and the only issue between the party is the amount of compensation. If the award is lower than the agreed minimum, then the defendant only need pay the lower limit; if the award is higher than the agreed maximum, the claimant will receive the upper limit. If the award falls within the agreed range, then the parties are bound by the actual award amount. Practice varies as to whether the figures may or may not be revealed to the tribunal, or whether the tribunal is even advised of the parties' agreement.
- Non-Binding Arbitration is a process which is conducted as if it were a conventional arbitration, except that the award issued by the tribunal is not binding on the parties, and they retain their rights to bring a claim before the courts or other arbitration tribunal; the award is in the form of an independent

assessment of the merits of the case, designated to facilitate an out-of-court settlement.

- Pendulum Arbitration refers to a determination in industrial disputes where an arbitrator has to resolve a claim between a trade union and management by making a determination of which of the two sides has the more reasonable position. The arbitrator must choose only between the two options, and cannot split the difference or select an alternative position. It was initiated in Chile in 1979 and has proved to be a very effective mechanism.
- This form of arbitration is also known as Baseball Arbitration. It takes its name from a practice which arose in relation to salary arbitration in Major League Baseball.
- Night Baseball Arbitration is a variation of baseball arbitration where the figures are not revealed to the arbitration tribunal. The arbitrator will determinate the quantum of the claim in the usual way, and the parties agree to accept and be bound by the figure which is closest to the tribunal's award.

Other Books on

MANAGEMENT

1.	Be a Better Project Manager (New)	125/-
2.	Be a Better Problem Solver (New)	125/-
3.	Be a Better Motivator (New)	125/-
4.	Be a Better Time Manager (New)	125/-
5.	Effective Director (New)	125/-
6.	Network Marketing (New)	150/-
7.	Art of Entrepreneurship (New)	125/-
8.	How to Beat Your Competitors	125/-
9.	How to Negotiate Effectively	125/-
10.	Make Your Boss Happy	125/-
11.	Art of Advertising	125/-
12.	Art of Marketing	125/-
13.	Art of Growing Business	125/-
14.	Art of Retailing	125/-
15.	Art of Leadership	125/-
16.	Art of Team Building	125/-
17.	Art of Corporate Communication	125/-
18.	Art of Organisational Management	125/-
19.	Improve your Marketing and Grow your Business	150/-
20.	What Customers Really Want	150/-
21.	Effective Presentation	150/-
22.	The Right Decision Every Time	150/-

23.	Develop Your Decision Making Skills	110/-
24.	Develop Your Team Building Skills	110/-
25.	Develop Your Skills to Conduct Effective Meetings	110/-
26.	How to Export And Import	95/-
27.	How to Use Money	95/-
28.	How to Start My Business	95/-
29.	How to Organise My Office	95/-
30.	How to Manufacture My Products	95/-
31.	How to Promote And Advertise	95/-
32.	How to Sell My Products	95/-
33.	How to Develop & Maintain Quality	95/-

Lotus PRESS

Unit No. 220, 2nd Floor, 4735/22,
Prakash Deep Building,Ansari Road, Darya Ganj,
New Delhi- 110002, Ph.: 32903912, 23280047, 09811594448
• E-mail : lotus_press@sify.com, www.lotuspress.co.in